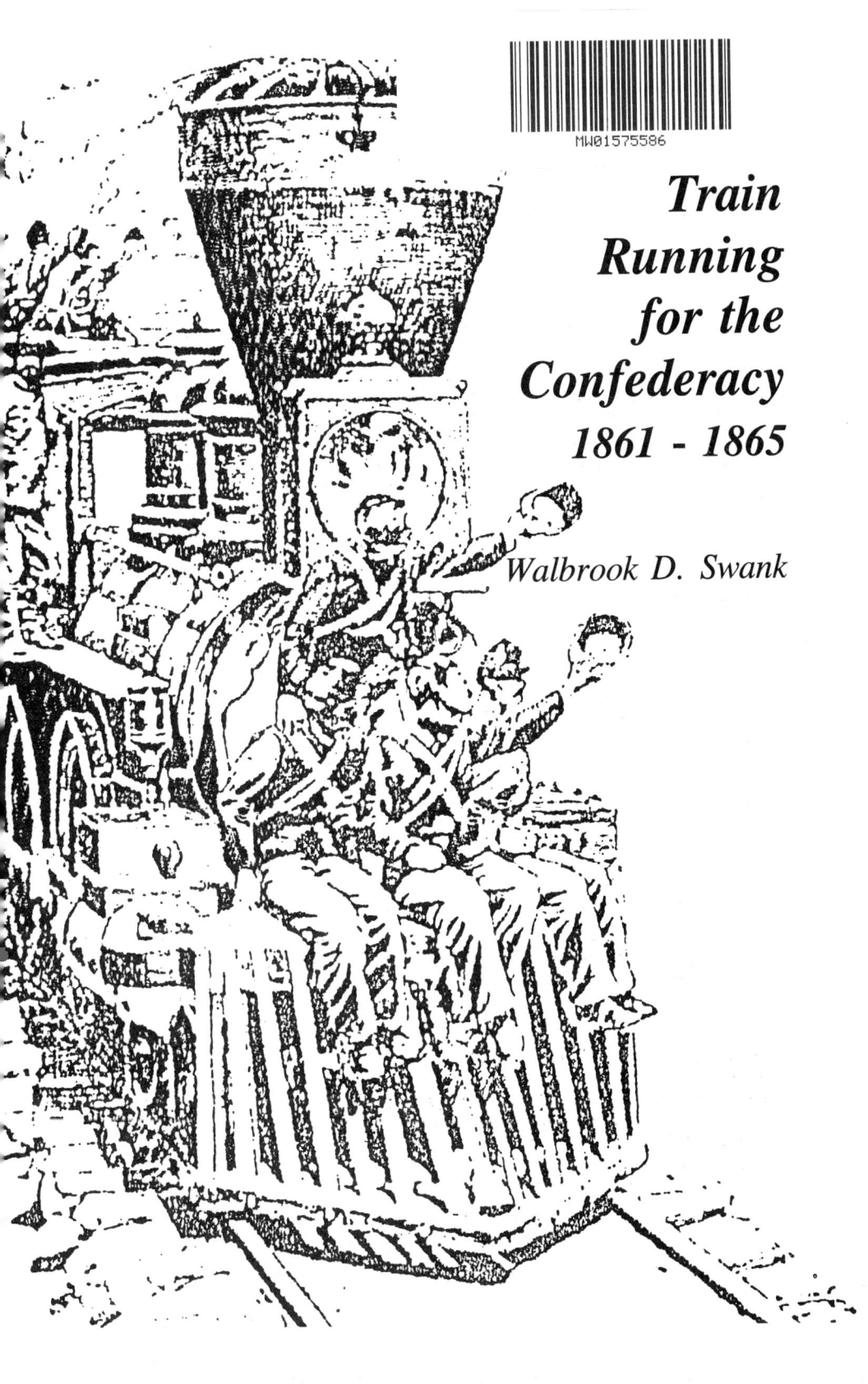

# Train Running for the Confederacy 1861 - 1865

*Walbrook D. Swank*

Cover Art:
From *Battles and Leaders of the Civil War*. Courtesy of Castle Books.

Copyright 1990
By Walbrook D. Swank and Carter and Pattie Cooke

Walbrook D. Swank, Colonel, USAF, Ret., Route 2, Box 433, Mineral, Virginia 23117

All rights reserved — no part of this book may be reproduced in any form without permission in writing from the publisher except by a reviewer who wishes to quote brief passages in connection with a review.

The acid-free paper used in this book meets the guidelines for permanence and durability of the Committee on Production Guidelines for Book Longevity of the Council of Library Resources.

Library of Congress Catalog Card Number:
90-90102

First Printing, 1990
Second Printing, 1991
Third Printing, 1992

ISBN 0-942597-42-7

First Printing by
Papercraft Printing & Design Company, Inc., Charlottesville, Virginia, U.S.A.

Second and Third Printing by
Burd Street Press, A Division of White Mane Publishing Co., Inc.,
Shippensburg, Pennsylvania, U.S.A.

For a complete list of available publications
please write
Burd Street Press
Division of White Mane Publishing Company, Inc.
P.O. Box 152
Shippensburg, PA 17257

# ABOUT THE AUTHOR

During his long career in the United States Air Force the author received numerous awards for meritorious service and at one time was a member of a Task Force in the Office of the Personnel Advisor to the President, The White House. Colonel Swank is a native of Harrisonburg, Virginia. His grandfather, Thomas S. Davis of Richmond, Virginia, was a member of the 10th Virginia Cavalry and a relative of President Jefferson Davis. Colonel Swank has written or edited three previous books about the North-South conflict, the last being his Award Winning *Confederate Letters and Diaries, 1861 - 1865.*

Colonel Swank has a Master's degree in American Military History and holds membership in the Bonnie Blue Society, which is based on his scholarly research and published literature. He is the recipient of the United Daughters of the Confederacy's Jefferson Davis Medal for his outstanding contributions to the preservation and promotion of our Southern history and heritage.

Among other organizations of which he is a member are the Military Order of the Stars and Bars, the Ohio State University Alumni Association and four Virginia historical societies.

Colonel Swank resides with his wife at "Walbrook," Frederick's Hall, Virginia.

## ACKNOWLEDGMENT

The writer wishes to express his deep appreciation to Pattie Cooke of Louisa, Va., for providing the material in this book. Carter S. Anderson, the author of these memoirs was the great, great uncle of Carter Cooke, her husband, who has graciously given permission to publish this fascinating work.

## DEDICATION

*To my parents, WILMER EDWARD SWANK and ARLINE DAVIS SWANK who instilled in me a deep appreciation for my southern heritage.*

# PREFACE

The strength of the railroad system of the Southern Confederacy was feeble in comparison with that of the North when guns opened fire in 1861. Of over 31,000 miles of rail lines in the United States before war broke out, only about 9,000 served the South. Southern railroads were hampered by weak iron rails, poorly constructed roadbeds, flimsy trestles, and poor maintenance. The typical train consisted of an eight wheel wood-burning engine of about twenty tons and about ten to twenty wooden cars. Some passenger trains had smaller locomotives and fewer cars.

During the War Between the States, Confederate railroads were key targets for attack and cavalry raids by Federal troops. The Virginia Central Railroad, that ran through battle-scarred Central Virginia, was a major transportation carrier of provisions, troops and war materials for General Robert E. Lee's Army. With only a few wood burning engines, generally poor and inadequate railroad rolling stock and with constant operating and maintenance problems, The Virginia Central Railroad performed yeoman service to the Confederate war effort. Historians have not given southern railroads the honor and recognition they deserve. This will become apparent to the reader as he views first-hand the trials and tribulations of a devoted southern trainman. Amidst the operations of this rail system, gunfire by Union and Confederate troops were often exchanged, collisions occurred, rail cars were raided and burned and drunkenness was common among trainmen and soldiers alike, as the rail cars moved along the tracks. Involved in many of these actions was a trainman on this key railroad. Because of his knowledge of these wartime activities he was asked to write about his fascinating, and often agonizing, experiences. This he did in a series of stories which were written during the period 1892–1894.

Excerpts from this fascinating narrative about train running for the Confederacy are presented here. Railroad and Civil War buffs will particularly enjoy this action-packed memoir of wartime railroading.

# SUFFICIENTLY TESTED

In 1864, the Confederacy needed a railway locomotive. A band of 100 men was selected from Lee's army and put under the command of a 6'4" Georgian, formerly a foreman of a stone quarry. The men went into Maryland and tore up a section of B&O Railway tracks, enabling them to capture the next train. With nothing except rope, those 100 men carried the locomotive 52 miles across streams, over hills, through bogs, into and out of woods. When they struck a line heading south, they ran the engine down to Virginia. President Garrett of the B&O could not believe the feat until he personally inspected the route taken with the locomotive. He declared the feat the most wonderful engineering ever accomplished. After the War, he searched for and located the Georgian leader of the band. On the basis of that single action, Garrett made him roadmaster of his entire system of railroads, saying, "Any man that can pick up an engine with fishing lines and carry it over a mountain has passed his examination with me."

# REMARKS OF ERNEST BATKINS, AN ASSOCIATE OF CARTER ANDERSON
## Written June 20, 1949

  Mr. C.S. Anderson was storekeeper at 17th Street storeroom, located near the shops, Richmond, Va., when I was messenger boy at "W" Telegraph Office, located near the west portal of Church Hill Tunnel, in 1900. One of my duties was to deliver him telegrams for which he had to sign for. He signed "CSA". The old gentleman, as I remember, had a ruddy complexion, long whiskers and was bowlegged. In that year there were two local trains running between Richmond and Gordonsville—numbered 29 and 30. No. 29 (westbound) would pick him up at the storeroom and let him off at Ashcake. No. 30 (eastbound) would pick him up at Ashcake and let him off at the storeroom. He always brought his lunch in a straw basket. These same trains were also used by Mr. Henry T. Wickham, former Vice-President and General Counsel, who carried his familiar "black bag."

  I understand some of Mr. Anderson's relatives live in his old home at Ashcake. Mr. Wickham's home is at Wickham, Va.

# INTRODUCTION

Carter S. Anderson, or "CSA", was born on a farm in Louisa County, Va., on Christmas Day, 1837, being educated at an Old Field School. On March 1, 1858, he came to the Virginia Central to assist W.H. Cosby who was then Agent at Ivy, Va. On June 10, 1860, Mr. Anderson, by this time a baggage master, made his first trip over the road from Richmond to Jackson's River, the then western terminus of the road. Jackson's river was approximately ten miles east of Covington, Va.

Mr. Anderson was made a regular passenger conductor in September, 1862, on the first accommodation train running between Richmond and Gordonsville. After the war, in May, 1865, he was made conductor of the mail train from Richmond to Covington, Va., to which latter point the road had been extended as of July 31, 1867. On the very first passenger train into Covington, Mr. Anderson was conductor.

The Virginia Central became the Chesapeake and Ohio Railroad Company as of August 31, 1868, with E. Fontaine still president. As of November, 1868, General Wms. C. Wickham became president. In 1869 C.P. Huntington and associates came into control of the road and under President Huntington construction was completed to the Ohio River in 1873. Mr. Anderson had been appointed paymaster in November, 1871, and he served until 1873, when he became chief clerk to Chief Engineer W.M.S. Dunn. In 1890 Mr. Anderson assumed the duties of storekeeper in Richmond, in addition to his being agent at his home station, Ashcake, Va., during the period 1885–1912.

It is said that in switching cars on the Richmond yards, the clerks and other yard men in chalking up the cars for distribution, got into the habit of associating the store room with Mr. Anderson, instead of Mr. Anderson with the store room, and the cars were chalked up "CSA"—(Confederate States America) instead of "store room".

Mr. Anderson retired on his seventy-fifth birthday, December 25, 1912, while Mr. George W. Stevens was President. During his entire lifetime his railroad came first; his loyalty was contagious, being shared by his family. On January 20, 1918, at the age of eighty-one, Mr. Anderson boarded a train for the Great Beyond.

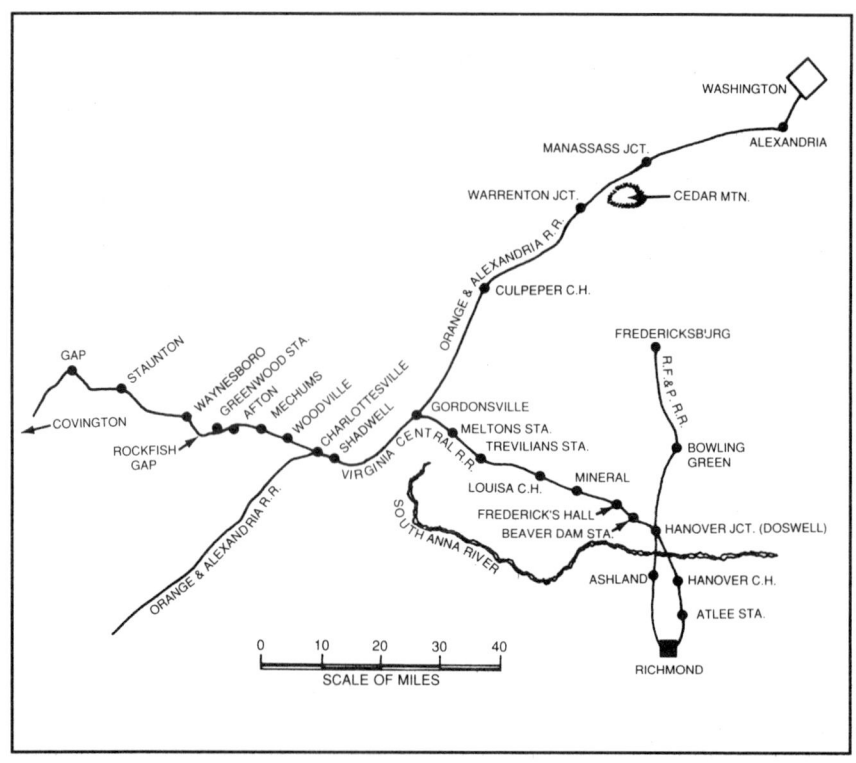

## UNION ARMY RAIDS ON VIRGINIA RAILROAD STATIONS, CONFEDERATE DEPOTS AND ADJACENT COMMUNITIES.

1862    Frederick's Hall by 2d N.Y. Cavalry of Gen. John Pope's Army of the Potomac.

1863    Gen. George Stoneman's Cavalry Force:
- Tolersville (Mineral)
- Louisa C.H.
- Frederick's Hall Station
- Ashland
- Hanover
- Beaver Dam

1864    Col. Ulric Dahlgren Cavalry Force under Gen. Judson Kilpatrick:
- Frederick's Hall Station
- Bumpass Turnout
- Beaver Dam Depot

Gen. Philip Sheridan's Cavalry Corps:
- Trevilian Station
- Louisa C.H.
- Ashland Station

1865    Waynesboro

# CONTENTS

### Chapter I
Moving General Lee's Men to Join Jackson
in the Valley......................................page 1

### Chapter II
Jackson Joins Lee in the Fight
Around Richmond, Virginia, 1862...............page 8

### Chapter III
The Trains Return After Delivering Troops, 1862......page 14

### Chapter IV
Locomotives Climb Broad Street Hill
in Richmond, Virginia, 1862...................page 25

### Chapter V
On the Move Toward the Valley.....................page 30

### Chapter VI
From Richmond on a Soldier Train.................page 38

### Chapter VII
Railroading at Waynesboro and Staunton, Virginia......page 43

### Chapter VIII
The Blues Close In................................page 48

### Chapter IX
Railroading Through the Raids.....................page 54

### Chapter X
Raids Around Richmond, Virginia..................page 59

### Chapter XI
Hanover Courthouse, Virginia, is Raided............page 67

# CHAPTER I

# Moving General Lee's Men to Join Jackson in the Valley

I will try to tell you something of the part the Virginia Central Railroad—now the Chesapeake and Ohio—performed in 1862 in moving a division of General Lee's army from Richmond to join General Jackson in the Valley of Virginia, and then bringing the whole army thus combined under Jackson along down and placing it in the rear of General McClellan.

To commence: General McClellan had swung around in the Chicahominy until he tapped our Virginia Central and Richmond, Fredericksburg and Potomac railroads, and had destroyed the South Anna River bridges on both roads. This caught some of our railroad men in Richmond and a good many of our engines, cars and men were out on the long end. Those of us who were caught in Richmond were at once put into the militia, doing local duty about the city.

I remember the first day we were out in sight of the Blue, that is, the northern troops, as we were stationed on Strawberry Hill. Then we were put at Young's mill and then east of Richmond, where we were put on picket duty on the Darbytown road. My beat was right alongside of the road, and from six to twelve, the password being "Geo. Washington."

Everything was quiet until about nine o'clock, when I heard a footstep firm and regular. My musket was at once brought to bear in that direction, when I remembered just in time that my first duty was to call "Who Goes There?" I now did this with all the dignity of a railroad Confederate soldier.

The traveler, who was an old darky, replied, "Hy! What this gwine on here now? Dis de fust time I beem ever ax fur a pass since I been had Liddy at Miss Jane Darby's and dat been ever sence four years arter de stars fell in thirty-three and two years arter Mrs Josephus brought Miss Delia home. Young boss, is y'awl our folks or is y'awl de Yankees?"

I answered him that he couldn't see Liddy that night but to go home. The old fellow retracted his steps muttering that "t'was a mighty bad sign." I never saw him again.

My time was out at twelve o'clock and I very soon, without any preliminaries, such as devotions, etc., measured my full length on the soft, wet pine tags, and resting my weary head between the projecting roots of a pine tree, was soon sleeping soundly and sweetly as those alone can sleep who have nobly saved their country (!). Some great man once said that the three noblest words in our language were: "Do your duty," but I, as well as our great men, do my own thinking, and there are only two plain little words I like better, "Duty done."

I awoke to hear the news that we were ordered to town and that all Virginia Central Railroad men must report at once to our Superintendent. Upon reaching our office, corner of Seventeenth and Broad Streets, Richmond, we received orders from Colonel H.D. Whitcomb, our general superintendent, who had proceeded up to Charlottesville, to report to him there, having left passes for us via the Richmond and Danville, South Side, and Orange, Alexandria and Manassas Railroads. We arranged accordingly and left early the next morning, having as our fellow passengers, on ours, and other sections of the Richmond and Danville troop trains, about 12,000 of Lee's men. When we reached Charlottesville we found that Colonel Whitcomb had already collected there everything that could turn a wheel on that end of the road, and ordered us to arrange crews to suit ourselves. He remarked that, in consideration of the enormous task of moving such an army with so limited a power, he would be glad to have one sober man in each crew, and that he had best not put all the whiskey men together. The solid, firm and feeling manner in which he said this had the effect he doubtless desired. The detachment sent from Lee to Jackson had no time to lose and demanded immediate transportation and listened to no excuse.

I remember well that hot June day we loaded the troops at the old Lynchburg Junction of the Virginia Central Railroad near the University of Virginia. Our cars were very rough, the most of our coaches were in Richmond and we had only freight cars, work-train flats, caboose cars and such as were scattered about on that portion of the road. The soldiers, and officers especially, complained heavily and curses thick and fast fell upon us as we worked and sweated to get them loaded. All at once in a loud tone bawled out a Confederate officer to our Superintendent, "You railroad men are a set of blockheads." It fired my young blood. Colonel Whitcomb's answer was indeed like "apples of gold in pitchers of silver." Said he, as he stood, coat off, in the broiling sun: "Well, sir, if we are blockheads, we are trying to do our duty." His noble answer satisfied the brave Confederate, who returned the soft answer, "Well, I suppose you are doing the best you can."

This little spat made us all, soldiers and railroad men, friends together, and we soon had everything on board and moving along our serpentine track about the base of those little ragged mountains between the University and Ivy Creek. Everything was serene, and not a murmur did we hear as the cool and refreshing mountain breezes fanned our heated, weary and hungry bodies. In a few hours the whole detachment was with General Jackson, who had reached Mechum's River with a large part of his Valley army. We received orders from General Jackson at once, after unloading our Richmond troops, to run through the Blue Ridge tunnel and bring him the remainder of his army. We had to go right on, and about daybreak the next morning we ran out of Blue Ridge tunnel and discovered at once our passengers as they lay along the little valley that runs parallel to the present C&O Railway between the Blue Ridge tunnel and where Basic City now stands—(that is, Waynesboro). We whistled and rang in order to wake the soldiers and get them aboard, which they very gladly and promptly did. We took them on, carefully running our trains back to Mechum's River. As soon as we reached there we found that everything there was on the move back to Charlottesville, which we had so hurriedly left. Then commenced the funniest experience of my life, for about two or three weeks, as well as I remember. (I am writing entirely from memory.)

All was curiosity and speculation as to the movement of the army. We had thought that Lee was re-enforcing Jackson in the Valley so that he could go on to Washington, a belief which lost but little force when we turned back from Mechum's River, as we concluded that

Washington could be reached more easily from Charlottesville than from the Valley. All the cavalry and artillery took the country roads, and a large part of the infantry. The army used our trains.

When we reached Charlottesville we had orders to unload, but very soon those we unloaded going on and those in rear coming walking up, we reloaded the tired ones and got orders to take them to Gordonsville. "Ah! I told you so," was in every mouth. "To Washington from Gordonsville is the nearest route of all." So it was. Well, the whole army got together there, or nearly all of it. It seems to me we stayed at Gordonsville a day or two. While there we received orders to head our trains all toward Washington and load them. Of course, then all doubts were removed, and all the subordinate officers, soldiers and railroad men fully believed that Jackson was going to Washington. The trains stood loaded all day; some of us pulled down a mile or two toward Orange Courthouse. Toward night, however, we got orders to unload and get our trains all back to Gordonsville.

Suddenly, very early the next morning, we were aroused by our Agent, Mr. Addison Gooch, rattling his stick along the outside of the cars in which we slept. He informed us that he had orders to tell the men that every engineer who was not ready to move his train in forty-five minutes would be shot. The wood which we used was very poor stuff with which to start a fire, being not much more than half seasoned and four-foot wood at that, which we had loaded on our tenders from the ricks as we came along on the road. But of all the impromptu inventions to increase heat and make the "pot boil," that morning's experience took the "rag off the bush." In making up our crews at Charlottesville, it fell to my lot to have for my engineer, John W. Whalley, running the little Roger engine named "Monroe." (The Annual Report lists the locomotive "Monroe" as built by Tredegar Works, placed on road in 1854. John Wesley, a gingerbread free negro, was firing for him. Mr. Whalley couldn't get steam on "Monroe", all he could do. He got mad with John Wesley, and it got John out of sorts, and it looked as though the Monroe got mad, too, and would not burn her wood nor steam at all. It began to be serious.

Every other train but ours was ready and the officers gathered around watching anxiously and very suspiciously our movements, and I found out that some suspicion had arisen as to Whalley's loyalty, his pedigree not being known to any of our people. I felt sorry for Whalley. He and I had made many a trip together under trying circumstances and he had many a time saved me from a whipping taking my part. He was a powerfully built man and fully six feet, six inches tall. I hunted around and found some old barrels in the rear of the depot, one of them an old tar barrel. I knocked them to pieces, and Samuel Wood, Brakeman, and myself got the barrels on the engine. Just as I stepped on the footboard I saw Mr. Whalley open his box and get all of his waste and pour on it all the oil he had and put it in. He then rolled in the old barrel staves. She began to roar. He took courage and looked around for any and everything that would make the fire burn the wood that was choked into the firebox. I saw Whalley take up the cushion on which he sat when running, and poke it into the firebox. It was very greasy and added much to the fire. Whalley then seemed to forget himself. He had as fine clothes as any man on the road but when he was running on his engine he did undoubtedly wear the greasiest clothes any mortal ever saw. Whalley had taken off his coat and laid it on the box in place of the cushion which he had burned. He snatched the coat and his pants to follow suit. But John Wesley, his fireman, said, "Mars Whalley, don't do dat; here's my coat," and in he dashed it. When the gauge of the Monroe in a few minutes showed 140 pounds of steam, the officers took off their hats and waved them and shouted, "Hurrah for Whalley and Monroe!"

Our trains were now all ready loaded and headed eastwardly. Orders came to go to Louisa Courthouse, and no further unless ordered by the Government and on their own responsibility. Then began again speculation, betting and argument indescribable, as to what Jackson was going to do or where on earth he was going. We reached Louisa in a few hours and unloaded all the troops. In fact, it seems that nearly all the army there got together and lay camped around and below Louisa Courthouse. The opinion seemed to prevail that it was nearer from Louisa Courthouse to Washington than from Gordonsville (and, by the way, there is not much difference), and that Jackson had decided to come down from Gordonsville to Louisa Courthouse and to go from there to Washington. This was the prevailing belief among the subordinate officers, soldiers and railroad men.

We remained at Louisa Courthouse several days, including one Sunday, and a memorable Sunday it was. Our trains lay east and west of Louisa, covering about four miles of main track. We had to leave space between trains in those days to pump up, the valuable injectors we now use not then being known or rather we had none. Everything was quiet, nothing seemed to be going on except there was reported a great religious revival among the soldiers who were then encamped in the groves below the Courthouse. Sunday morning all of us railroad men gathered around the telegraph office at Louisa to try to hear what could be done. We had no rations, scarcely, and there were so many soldiers about that it was impossible to buy anything to eat. By twelve o'clock noon more than half of the railroad men were drunk. We drank during the war mostly new apple brandy, and it is a very hot and firey dram. A great many of the soldiers and the subordinate officers had come to town too and gotten drunk, and it was the jolliest crowd at the depot you ever saw. All at once—squeel-squell! loud, long and distressingly, we heard an engine coming from toward Richmond. We could not understand what on earth it could be, as we had with us every engine we had. "It must be a Yankee engine pulling McClellan's troops," said everyone. It was soon found out, however, that some official had run the gauntlet from Richmond and had gotten a little RF&P engine that happened to be outside of Richmond, and a little coach, and was making his way to Charlottesville.

The urgent request came to us to move all of our trains far enough to allow the little courier train to make the siding at Louisa and then back down east of Louisa until she could turn out of the west end of the switch. But, "here's the rub!" More than half of us were drunk, every engine cold, nobody knew anything, nor had anybody seen anybody else. It was with the greatest effort on the part of all who had sense enough to appreciate our situation that we got the trains far enough west to let the courier train in, and then about the same trials to get them back down below the Courthouse, so that the little courier train could get out the west end and go on to Charlottesville. It took the best part of the day to get the track clear. In the meantime, it took so long for us to get the track open that the messenger man had either gone to see some of the officers or was getting his dinner, so that all of the railroad men and thousands of idle soldiers had gathered around to examine, criticize and find out all about this crew and its errand. My engineer Whalley, was pretty drunk.

He went around and chinned the little engine, made a great many ridiculous remarks about her, and finally bet twenty dollars that he could hold the little engine with ten men and could thus prevent her moving until he said so. Knowing the importance of the occasion, I begged Whalley not to attempt such a thing, it was too serious, but the soldiers told him to go ahead. Somebody took the bet and Whalley selected his men.

Presently here came the messenger, got upon the coach and told his engineer, "Go to Charlottesville; minutes are hours!" About twenty strong men dropped their strength against the coach. "Chow, chow, chow, spow, spow, spow!" went the little engine. I feared every minute that I would hear a shot. The engineer made several vain trials, and seeing his point gained, Whalley said, "Give her a push, boys, and let her go." And off she shot amid the loud cheers of the soldiers. It was the most ridiculous sight I ever witnessed.

I have taken so many sidings that I have failed to make my terminal, and I will have to stop and wait until you give me right of track to finish my trip. How we took those 30,000 troops and placed them within a day's march of McClellan's rear, moving with muffled whistles and bells off the engines—of this I will tell in another letter, if I find time.

# CHAPTER II

## Jackson Joins Lee In the Fight Around Richmond, 1862

Taking up the narrative of the part performed in the summer 1862 by the Virginia Central, now C&O, in transferring General Jackson's army from the Valley of Virginia and placing them in a position to attack General McClellan's rear, while the Johnston-Lee army attacked McClellan in front, I now proceed. My last letter left us at Louisa Courthouse, Sunday night, with not even a rumor of any movement. It was so quiet and peaceful we forgot it was the time of war. On Monday morning though the scene changed. If any of General Jackson's officers knew where he was going they were extremely true and prudent in keeping his plans secret. I have no intention of attempting to write war history, neither does General Jackson's characteristic tactics need anything from my humble pen; but I will make one remark which is as applicable to success in business as well as to success in war. General Jackson undoubtedly used the enemies spies. He was glad for them to see and tell everything he was doing. Then he always did the opposite of what the average person would think logical and advisable—therefore likely. That was certainly true of him in this movement, for on Monday morning he had everybody, citizens and soldiers, figuring out the nearest and best roads to Washington. The railroad men felt confident we would not soon have any more soldiers. Before noon, however, the lumbering of heavy artillery could be heard along the country roads toward Richmond and everything wore a serious and somber aspect. Pretty soon our orders came to prepare immediately every train. The orders were sharp; "Load every train to fullest capacity; let each train give preceding train thirty minutes time. Keep trains well in hand. Sound no whistle; ring no bell. Brakeman, keep a sharp lookout for trains in front and rear. Death to whole crew who cause a collision!" This was indeed what might be called a "limited time card".

Our Superintendent (Whitcomb), acting under instructions of President Edmund Fontaine, then living in Richmond, would not assume the responsibility of running his trains any further into our unoccupied territory but was perfectly willing to allow the government to use the trains on its own responsibility. Since McClellan had removed the line of battle from Manassas to the Peninsula, beautiful Piedmont had been unoccupied by either army. Anywhere from the Potomac to the James, and east of the Blue Ridge to Richmond, the citizens would just as soon have expected one army as the other! The Southern, as well as the Northern, officers in approaching a farm house would note that awful stillness around and the apparent absence of every occupant of a once happy lovely home. "Halloo" would strike such terror into the souls of the unprotected women and children and cowardly men hiding within that in many cases actual death resulted. For once the rich and the poor met together and sweet life was all they asked for: "only this and nothing more."

So, no wonder our engineers hesitated to plunge their trains into such a situation. On the night the above orders were received the rain was pouring and darkness was thick. The engineers of the trains gave no thought to their own lives. But each one felt the responsibility of 2,000 soldiers, the average on each of the ten trains. The officers were very kind to us and reassured us by saying that our cavalry had gone all through the country as low as the South Anna River and there was not a Yankee soldier west of Hanover Courthouse. Furthermore, they gave us two Confederate officers who rode on the pilot of the engine on the front train.

Our ten trains of eighteen and twenty cars per train were very soon placed for loading. I wish our passengers nowadays could have seen how quickly (about ten minutes it was) 1500 to 2000 men with their heavy muskets, clumsy shoes and haversacks crawled into and on top of twenty box cars and work train flats. There is perhaps wisdom in letting every man have a little taste of war. I know that war is the finest "peace tonic" I ever took. I don't know how you northerners feel, but down here our old veterans made the best of citizens in a united country. They have seen a-plenty.

Well, to my story: Conductor John H. Richardson and Engineer Martin Alley took the load of the ten trains on this momentous occasion and two safer men never pulled a bell cord or stepped upon a footboard, Martin looking very serene in his cab of the Westward Ho (Built by Rogers Bros. and placed on road in 1857)—a Confederate brigadier on either wing of his pilot. It was a war picture indeed, and as he quietly and carefully pulled his engine pin and drew his train into the curve east of Louisa, there went up a yell from the boys that filled the whole air around us. My train came next and my engineer, John Whalley, was signaled to pull down in place to load. To my horror, I discovered that John was drunk, and that my fireman, John Wesley, was dead drunk! We needed but little steam, however, as it was mostly down grade all the way.

I hope I may never again experience such feelings as I then had. I had on board 2,000 soldiers, a train just ahead, one immediately in the rear; overloaded, pouring rain, nearly night, engineer in liquor, no fireman; not a whistle allowed to be sounded, not a bell allowed to be rung! At once I held an earnest conversation with Conductor Joshua Finks and Engineer Fendal Ragland in charge of train immediately behind mine. No kinder man ever lived than Josh Finks. He was much older than I, and putting his arm around my trembling shoulders, said: "Carter, get on your engine and keep John from running into Richardson and Ragland and I will keep from running into you." I gratefully acted as he suggested and stepping upon the Monroe", my engine, in front, tied a knot in the whistle cord, remembering the order "No whistle." Cautioning my brakeman to keep a sharp lookout for my signals from my lamp on the engine, and to use the brake on Whalley if he wanted to run too fast, I then informed Mr. Whalley that we were ready. He stepped upon the Monroe's footboard, and stooping a little to enter his cab, he tapped her open in his characteristic way. I sat on the box opposite him and watched anxiously the curves as we rolled gently along toward Mineral City. He then told the fireman, John Wesley, to fill her up, at the same time opening the firebox door with the toe of his boot. Wesley was so drunk that he mistook the wood in the tender for the

## WESTWARD HO LOCOMOTIVE

Picture taken at Winifrede Junction, W. Va., 1870.

Built by Rogers Locomotive Works.
Placed on road July, 1857.
Cylinders, 15 x 22"
Weight in tons, 27½
Diameter of drivers, 66"
No. of drivers, 4
Dimensions of firebox, 51 x 39 x 60"
No. of flues, 141
Diameter of flues, 2"
Length of flues, ft. and inches, 11.4
Diameter of boiler, 43"
Service, first mail, later passenger.

(Quoted from 1857 Virginia Central Annual Report. Page 12).

The Westward Ho was the second of that name on the railroad. The first was built by Norris Brothers, placed on road in 1848, when the road was still called the Louisa Railroad (1836-1850). Disposed of in 1856.

In picture the engineer is Andy Southworth; the fireman is Bernard (Barney) Hagan, standing with tallow pot in hand.

Courtesy of John B. Gilmer, Louisa, Va.

firebox and began cramming wood back and firing the tender! We were now approaching the 65 feet per mile grade east of Mineral City and we had gotten into a pretty good swing on the level. I knew there was great danger. I asked Whalley to shut her off and get the train well in hand before he struck the grade. His eye flashed fire. He snatched the Monroe's throttle wide open and as she struck the down grade, we dashed through Rock Cut at a desperate speed. Physically, I was nothing to Whalley, but fear left my timid frame and gave me strength instead. I felt I could do anything! I snatched the stick out of Whalley's hand and whatever I had to do, I would do, and reached immediately for the whistle cord, forgetting that it was death to pull it. The cord I had tied, however, saved his life. He at once drew her in back gear and as soon as he possibly could do so, nearly stopped the train.

Looking ahead as we entered the reverse curve, I exclaimed: "Great God Whalley, just look!" There, just ahead of us, on the curve near Frederick's Hall, was what I had been dreading for the last few minutes, the red lights on the rear of Richardson's train as he slowly and cautiously rolled down the grade. Whalley realized now the situation. It sobered him. With tears rolling rapidly out of his great eyes, he beckoned me to come out on the ground to him and drawing me close to him told me that when he shut off the Monroe and reversed her, it was with the full determination to throw me into the fire-box, and the only thing that stopped him was the ruby glare from the rear of Richardson's train! This was narrow escape from such an awful wholesale massacre as would inevitably have followed, had Whalley not shut off when he did that it completely sobered him and well it might. We crept along to Frederick's Hall and putting a brakeman to firing, I took his place on the top of the rear car and we reached the end of our trip in good order but drenched with rain.

General Jackson did not take the train at all but generally kept ahead of us. He stopped overnight at Frederick's Hall at the hospitable home of Mr. N.W. Harris. (The son of Frederick Harris, first President of Louisa Railroad, for whom Frederick Hall station is named. The Louisa Railroad, 1836–1850, was predecessor of Virginia Central Railroad). Mrs. Harris assigned General Jackson her best room, and, the family retiring, Jackson slipped out and left for Richmond about

45 miles by the nearest route. He held a council of war with President Jefferson Davis, General Lee and others and returned to Mrs. Harris' to breakfast. Being a little late he apologized for it, remarking that he often took moderate horseback exercise before breakfast! Mrs. Harris' maid was much bewildered to find that the general's bed had not been touched and ran down to tell Mrs. Harris that "De gen'l slep on de flo' or he made up de bed hisself."

Mrs. Harris was curious to know how it happened but when she went to ask him the silent old war horse was gone.

*Note: The story of Jackson's visit to Frederick Hall is related in history and fiction, in the biographies of Jackson and in "The Long Roll" by Mary Johnston. General Jackson arrived at Frederick's Hall from the Valley on his way to Richmond, Sunday was spent at camp meeting. He made the Frederick's Hall house his headquarters while waiting for his army to come up on the Virginia Central train with the advance guard. That night he spent at Frederick Hall and during the night; with his aid, Major Robert Lewis Dabney, he departed for Richmond without telling anyone his destination. According to Malcolm H. Harris, in his "History of Louisa County," Mrs. Harris sent her servant to ask the general to breakfast and finding his body servant, asked for the General, to which the servant replied that the General left during the night. This neighborhood was a busy place during those years. Custer had his headquarters here during his raid with Sheridan in 1864.*

# CHAPTER III

# The Trains Return After Delivering Troops 1862

Closing my last letter, we were rolling along that dark and rainy night about Frederick's Hall with our ten trains of about twenty cars each, all loaded inside and outside with Jackson's soldiers going —none of us knew where—except that our orders were to go to Beaver Dam, which is forty miles from Richmond, and about twenty-five miles from where it might have been supposed some of General McClellan's men would be scouting. We got orders, just as soon as we pulled up to Beaver Dam, to unload and pull down east a mile or so, to allow the eight rear trains to come up to the stations. This threw us down in the woods a mile and a half.

Just as soon as our next neighbor—the following train—came up to us, Engineer Whalley got his engine cooled and came on back to our caboose—a wet and muddy freight car. We were down side by side on the floor and fast asleep sooner than I can write it down. Mortal was never happier than I was on being relieved of such responsibility. The sun was climbing up out of the tree-tops when we awoke. Being chilled from getting wet and the night air, we crawled up on top of the cars to dry and get warm, wondering what would be our next move. Whalley, my engineer, had no coat long, having thrown his in the firebox at Gordonsville to get his engine hot. He had drank right freely of new brandy the past day and being thoroughly drenched with the rain he got chilled so that he trembled awfully. He said he believed he would go up to the station and try to get a dram from some of the officers and hear what news he could. In half an hour or so he came back. I took him to be a Confederate officer, but soon discovered that Whalley had on a Confederate brigadier's coat. "Promoted!" he bawled out as he pulled up. He had gotten a good big drink and the officer happening to remember the circumstances of his being without a coat kindly gave him a really good Confederate officer's gray dress coat. He had it buttoned closely around his other wet and greasy clothes which made him a ridiculous sight.

"What news, John?"

"Plenty of it", he replied. "The men have orders to cook three days rations and prepare to march."

"Did you learn anything as to the direction they are going?" "Not positively," he answered, "but I begin to think that they are going to get into his scrimmage around Richmond because, when the officer gave me the coat, he remarked that where he was going it would be plenty hot without a coat."

Whalley had scarcely finished telling us this when we heard and soon saw the army moving along the County road, right along side the railroad, where the trains were standing. Conjectures fled, and the solution of the question as to where Jackson was going was solved. He was certainly on the Richmond road. The cavalry in front, artillery next, then the infantry, and some cavalry in the rear. Quietly—that is —no music, no shooting nor boisterous commands, but gleefully and cheerfully marched forward the whole of Jackson's command. Our soldiers loved to go and fight. It was camp that sickened and killed our boys. They longed to fight it out and go home. They cursed each delay and worshipped a dashing, daring leader. On, on, they passed: "Some to Fame; many wounded on the field to lie. A few to Shame, but most and best of them to die." The goodbyes given them as they passed along.

In a few hours there remained not a sign of any army about Beaver Dam. General Jackson left a respectful request for us not to sound the whistles until we got as far as Louisa Courthouse on our return. Being thus set free from military rule, we held council and decided upon getting back to our superintendent at Charlottesville. We had not been to bed nor eaten a regular, decent meal for nearly a fortnight. At that time, here in Virginia a soldier was everything and a man who was not in the army stood a poor show indeed, so long as there were any soldiers to be attended to. We were near the point of starvation. The engineers decided to examine their engines before starting on the return trip, as the engines would all have to go to

Charlottesville before they could be turned around. Tink, tink, tink, under or somewhere on every engine, could be heard the hammers and chisels. The engines had not been near a shop for a month or more, and it is a mystery now how those engineers did the work required to be done, and managed to keep their engines together.

It was arranged that returning the order of trains would be, "The last shall be first and the first shall be last." This placed in front Conductor D. Pat Woodward and Engineer Westley Huntley, who ran the mountain climber, "C.R. Mason's Baldwin" engine, placed on the road in 1854, built to take four passenger coaches down and up a grade of 360 feet to the mile, and it was used between Millboro tunnel and Mason's tunnel, where the Lick Run fill now is. Her tender was on top of her, or rather on each side and on top. She had no truck, but was built on four small drivers, and when working waddled about and switched herself from side to side. She was named for C.R. Mason, venerable contractor and engineer. We had her at that time in service on the main line, as engines were so scarce. The tender on top was not sufficient to hold water enough to go from tank to tank, and Master Mechanic Wildman had attached to her a captured B&O tender. She was the laughing stock of the party. It was discovered by Engineer Huntley that the Mason's drives were loose—a serious matter. Huntley hunted up Conductor Lex. Netherland, who usually carried along in his caboose from four to six tons of scrap, which he would pick up and say, "It will come in." Mr. Netherland had a barrel of charcoal and an old 20-gallon iron pot which was in those days used to hang on the rack and boil clothes in. He would build a coal fire in the pot, jab a piece into it, and using a track rail for his anvil, would do a pretty good blacksmith job. Conductor Netherland soon had his shop in full blast for tightening the drivers on the Mason. With the assistance of some of the older engineers, Huntley soon got her on her feet and took the lead.

We found an office open at Fredericks Hall and reported to Colonel H.D. Whitcomb, at Charlottesville, who ordered us to come to Gordonsville and report. We had nothing to meet and no cause to hurry, so we jogged along, occasionally seeing the rear of the preceding train. Passed Louisa, Trevillian, and struck out for Gordonsville. Our train had reached Forest Hill Church, about one and a half miles from Melton, when we were flagged down. "What's the matter ahead?"

Nobody could tell from the fact that everybody except the fireman on each train had gone ahead to find out just what caused the halt. Walking on ahead, we found the colored brakeman on the front train, which was standing with the engine at the tank at Melton, a water station four miles east of Gordonsville. "What's the matter, Tillman? Those drivers loose again?" Tillman answered, "No sir, Mars Pat and Mr. Huntley up dar at Harkless' shanty getting something to eat. Mr. Huntley done swore dat de Mason shall stand dar till the owls bill dar ness in her biler fore he'll tech her till he get something to eat."

We joined in "Amen." Harkless was one of two men who pumped water at Melton, and Melton being a place out of the way, no army had ever camped there and we very often stopped there and got Harkless to cook us something to eat. Harkless, who was a slave, had there accumulated a pretty good supply of ham, eggs, coffee, etc., and was patronized that day to his full capacity. Harkless had not sufficient table service to accommodate more than a crew or two at once and the boys would eat and fall back. Never was royal banquet enjoyed as was that strong, hot coffee, ham and eggs, and hot ash-cake, which Harkless baked on the large slate rocks of which the hearth was constructed.

We were about through eating, and getting ready oiling up, to go ahead, when an old citizen came walking down the track from Gordonsville, and as he came up to us, asked some of the men if they had heard the news, "What news?"..."Why, the Yankees are expected in Gordonsville before night. They say they are now at Orange Courthouse, on their way to Gordonsville."

What on earth to do we did not know. Engineer Ragland said he did not believe it, and would run his engine up there, or at any rate, in sight, and see, but it was thought best not to run any engine nearer for fear they would find out about so many trains being there. Well, Ragland said he would walk up there and see, and off he went, assuring us that he would be back soon if he did not get shot.

We waited and watched, until finding the day was nearly gone, we walked on up to meet Ragland or somebody else. We found him about a mile from Melton, sitting on the end of a tie, as tight as a tick. We approached him and earnestly begged him to tell us all about how it was at Gordonsville, but he imagined that he had told us, and would only reply that: "If you all know so much more than I do, it is no use for me to tell you. You can go up to Gordonsville and see for yourself, if you don't believe what I say."

We gave him up and were about arranging to send another squad this time to find out the state of affairs at Gordonsville when we saw someone coming, rapidly walking down the track from toward Gordonsville and soon recognized Mr. C.E. Wildman, master Mechanic.

"What on earth is the matter with you all, boys? Colonel Whitcomb is on his head, afraid you are all captured or wrecked. Where are your trains?

We informed him, and also of the rumors we had heard. He told us that there was a rumor that General Pope had crossed the Potomac and was operating toward the direction of Gordonsville but there was no immediate danger and that we should go on at once to Gordonsville and get orders to go right on to Charlottesville, which we did, and reached that place some time in the night.

Next morning we all went in a body and reported to our superintendent Colonel Whitcomb, who thanked and congratulated us, remarking that it was remarkable that not the slightest accident had occurred nor injury to any soldier, and that we could all rest that day, and that next morning he wanted the engineers to take their engines to Shadwell where Mr. Wildman had erected a temporary shop; and give them an overhauling, to be in readiness for the next campaign". So we decided to order breakfast at the Exchange Hotel for the whole party, about thirty men. Conductor Finks and Nat. Shepherd were appointed a committee to go up and arrange with the proprietor for a big breakfast, or whatever you might call it—it was early in the forenoon. By the time they got breakfast ready the most of the boys had drank their neighbor's health pretty freely, and a merry crowd it was, as we gathered around the perfectly white and clean table with hot smoking scratchbacks, coffee, and steak.

War is very demoralizing and it did seem to me that the men forgot everything else on earth but just making the most of that jolly hour. One grind on the steak was enough to satisfy the most carniverous that she was tough. Then began comparisons, anecdotes the most amusing and ridiculous, not to say any more. Captain D. Pat Woodward always was very touchy about any remarks being made which would cast any reflections on what he was eating. He was out of the ring pretty soon and others followed. Finally, Conductor Nat. Shepherd, who stammered miserably, raised the question: "What sort of meat is this, boys?" Answers came quickly from all around the table. Bull beef, calf, dog, mule, goat, wild boar. Nobody had any idea it was mutton. Shepherd bet it was mutton. "Done," said Whalley, "here's ten dollars if it is not."

Proof was called for by all. Shepherd held up a good chunk of the old ram on his fork and exhibiting to us a good bunch of wool, pulled in the money, remarking that he never saw that kind of hair grow on a calf.

Breakfast being over and paid for, we pulled for the rooms—the box cars. "Let's go a-fishing," met with no favorable response. I determined to go and buying a small quantity of tackle, was soon on the banks of the muddy Rivanna along where she seeks the shadows of Monticello to get herself in good shape before making her terminal flow into the James River.

I had scarcely a nibble; I studied the art of fishing; tried all sorts of bait, disliking so to go back empty-handed. I had gotten down opposite Jefferson's old Shadwell mills, hoping to find a hole where the fish would bite. I saw just ahead of me, under a bending willow, two little negro boys. As I came up to and made friends with them, I saw they were fishing, and they soon showed me how to do it. Snatching out a good-sized "cat", the larger of the boys pulled out of the bushes to hang this one on a bunch of fish which weighed at least ten pounds. The idea struck me at once to buy them out. They were soon made happy as to the trade, and giving them my hook and line, I struck out for Charlottesville, "big as life".

I exposed my luck to the best of my ability, being determined that every railroad man should know of my success, even to our unsuspecting superintendent. The fish were served for supper and my point gained. All hands were bent on going early and spending the next day on the Rivanna. Great preparations were made: bread, fryingpans, a two-gallon jug of brandy and abundant tackle. "Are you going along?" I was asked the next morning.

"No," I replied, "yesterday was fishing enough to satisfy me for the season; go on, boys, and success attend your efforts." They had planned a great fish fry at old Shadwell Mills.

I cannot describe the scene which appeared as those boys came along through the switches at Charlottesville yard, late in the afternoon, returning from their grand fishing excursion. Colonel Whitcomb had been let into the secret, and was so diverted from his usual dignity that the boys suspected me, and finally found it out. No power on earth could have kept us from laughing, but curses fell thicker and faster on me than ever before and since. They threatened me all sorts of punishment.

Whilst we were thus trifling precious time away, great military movements were being brought into action around Richmond. Next day, through all Piedmont district—in fact, taking Richmond as the center for about 100 miles around—could be heard the thunder, low muttering and now and then great blasts of artillery under the command of Generals McClellan, Lee and Jackson.

The historian has the floor as to that Seven Days' fight, and I must continue my railroad narrative. Flying rumors from Richmond were all favorable to our side, and Colonel Whitcomb energetically set to work organizing a large carpenter force to rebuild the burnt bridges between RF&P Junction — (now called Doswell) — and Richmond, resuming passenger service to Richmond via Richmond, Fredericksburg and Potomac Railroad from the Junction, and transferring passengers and baggage over South Anna bridge to the trains which came up to the burned bridge from Richmond.

The travel increased daily on our road. That from the southern roads to Richmond became enormous. The reports going out, exaggerated, of course, as to General McClellan's defeat, brought crowds to the city, refugees returning, parents to attend their wounded sons, and many sad ones seeking among the slain to recognize a lost brother or son—many times digging up from a two-foot grave their bodies to be carried home, to City Cemetery, or decently buried on the battlefield.

Being then baggage-master, my trip brought me to Richmond the night of the Battle of Malvern Hill. After supper I strolled out into Capitol Square. It had been reported all the afternoon that General McClellan had been surrounded, and his whole army prisoners, but the way those war dogs barked on Malvern Hill convinced us all that it was not true.

Capitol Square was literally packed. I remember there were a large number of beautiful and nicely dressed ladies, many of them strangers in the city, and for three or four hours, it seems to me now, we remained there listening to the thundering, bursting and terrific cannonading on Malvern Hill that hot, clear and starry night. Next morning it was known that General McClellan had gotten under cover of his gunboats and was safe.

There was now no doubt as to General Pope moving in the direction of Gordonsville and just as soon as General Lee could spare him he arranged to let General Jackson go to Gordonsville to meet General Pope, and President Edmund Fontaine and Superintendent Whitcomb were urged by the government to hurry the bridge so that the army could go directly back to Gordonsville in time to save, if possible, that very important military station. Then commenced to hustle indeed on the part of our railroad officials to connect the two ends of our road, get the machinery together, our engines to the shops, and to satisfy the great military pressure bearing on us for immediate transportation for Jackson's army to meet General Pope who was pressing toward Gordonsville.

George R. Thomasson, the veteran bridge builder of Virginia, and West Virginia, was at that time our master road carpenter and had full charge of rebuilding the bridges and trestling which General McClellan had destroyed between RF&P Junction (this was also called Hanover Junction) and Richmond. Acting under Superintendent Whitcomb's orders, he had organized a strong force of carpenters with work train, Conductor Horace Gooch, and a big force of laborers, a good engine and twenty flats to haul the timber, which was being prepared by a part of the carpenter force, whilst Mr. Thomasson and his best men were at the burned bridges removing the debris and preparing to rebuild. After the Seven Days' fight a great pressure was brought to bear on Thomasson. Colonel Fontaine, who was as much concerned about the immediate transportation of troops as he was about his road, he being a strong Confederate (he lost two sons in battle), took matters into his own hands. He instructed Mr. Thomasson to cut timber wherever he found it most convenient and suitable, that the patriotism of the people would allow this on account of the urgent necessities of the government for transportation.

George immediately threw a good force into the beautiful pine timber, about two miles east of South Anna, belonging to Mr. Wickham. Returning to the bridge he met Mr. Wickham walking down the track toward Hanover Courthouse, probably to get the news.

After speaking to Mr. Thomasson in his usual very polite manner, he halted to pass a few words in conversation with regard to the situation of things military and resuming business on the road. His quick ear soon caught the sound of axes as whack, whack, whack, they very well imitated cavalry pistols.

"Gracious God, Mr. Thomasson, what do I hear?" he remarked, as he straightened himself up, placing his hands on his sides, as he always did under excitement. "Is it not cavalry firing?"

"No, sir," answered Mr. Thomasson, "It is my men cutting pine piles to trestle South Anna bridge".

"In the name of God, Mr. Thomasson, by whose authority did you dare enter my premises?"

Mr. Thomasson told Mr. Wickham that Colonel Fontaine ordered him to do it, repeating to Mr. Wickham what Colonel Fontaine had said about the patriotism of the people, etc.

Mr. Wickham snatched the word patriotism out of Mr. Thomasson's mouth with "Patriotism, hell!" and Mr. Thomasson says he never heard cursing put into such grammatical sentences nor such beautiful words as Mr. Wickham laid on him. Mr. Wickham used as fine English as any gentleman in Virginia at that time, and under strong provocation could cuss. Extremes politically met in Mr. W.F.

Wickham, who was every inch an Old-Line Whig, and Colonel Edmund Fontaine, who was a Democrat, a "red hot rebel".

How these gentlemen made it with regard to the timber cutting I don't know, but Thomasson got the trees and built the bridges. Colonel Fontaine went to another extreme in his eagerness to get his road open. He ordered Road Master William Richardson to bring at once every section-hand east of Gordonsville and let the foremen walk and watch their track. This did not work because the raw section hands knew nothing about bridge building and the carpenters were afraid to allow them on the bridge to any extent. Mr. Thomasson had the bridges and trestling all up and Mr. Richardson had the track replaced where it was torn up in a remarkably short time, considering the extent of the damage. The track in some places was actually turned over.

Just think of it. These Northern soldiers would go on a moderate embankment, generally on a curve, and raise the track until it would turn over completely, bottom-side up, and some parts of it setting up like a fence. They knew we were scarce of rails and would pile up cross ties, then lay the rails across the pile, set fire to it, and when the rails got red hot, seize them at both ends, with rail tongs, and twist them around the trees, leaving them looking like great snakes.

When the order came to haul Jackson's army to Gordonsville, to meet General Pope about August 1, 1862, our road was open and we did not let anybody walk back but gave them all a ride, and having gotten our rolling stock together, once more we had the pleasure of giving our soldiers rather better accommodations than we could when we brought them down.

*Note: In the Annual Report for 1862 (pages 11–12) the following account of injury to the road by the enemy appears: "During the past summer (1862) a portion of the road between Hanover Courthouse and Richmond was in the hands of the enemy. They did no great injury either to the roadway or any other property of the Company, except the burning of South Anna bridge. A few rails were torn up in several places and two pieces of trestle work and a few freight cars were burnt. This forebearance is doubtless to be ascribed to the fact that* they confidently expected in a short time to be in possession of the City of Richmond and the whole road and consequently only aimed to impair its immediate usefulness to us. The bridge across the South Anna, for want of time, was repaired and constructed of trestle work. Its strength and present safety is undoubted...All the buildings at Beaver Dam and the bridge across the Cowpasture River were also destroyed by the enemy with fire. Depot at Beaver Dam has been rebuilt and almost completed."

General Superintendent H.D. Whitcomb reported on the enemies' activities in the 1862 Annual Report, page 26: "On May 19 the enemy took possession of Jackson's River Depot, and a detachment of cavalry piloted by W.P. Rucker, formerly a citizen of Alleghany County, proceeded as far as the Cowpasture bridge and burned it..."

"In last May the enemy occupied the road at or near Atlee's station. (Near Richmond). A few days afterward they occupied Hanover Courthouse, and the road from Chickahominy to South Anna river remained in their possession until their defeat before Richmond, June 29. During this time they burned the South Anna bridge and the trestles near Hanover Courthouse and on Mrs. Crenshaw's farm. They also destroyed seven cars and their contents. The track was torn up in several places and most of the negroes employed by the Company were carried away.

"As soon as possible; after the road was cleared, we commenced the necessary repairs, and completed them by July 18. A substantial trestle was built over South Anna in place of the bridge...

"On July 20 the enemy visited Beaver Dam station and destroyed the buildings and contents. On August 6 they visited Frederick's Hall station and fired some of the buildings and one car, but spared the depot on account of its proximity to a private dwelling. The government stores in the depot were destroyed. In both these cases the enemy left in a short time."

"The locomotive Monroe exploded on November 19, 1862, killing Assistant Yardmaster Davis..." 1862 Annual Report.

# CHAPTER IV

# Locomotives Climb Broad Street Hill in Richmond, 1862

The stormy and terrific battle of Malvern Hill, which was fought at night, closed the Seven Days' fight. General McClellan, under cover of the gun-boats lying in the James River, arranged for a Bay Line voyage to Washington, while our people had their hands full burying the dead and caring for the wounded...A few days before the Seven Days' fight General McClellan had destroyed all the bridges on the Virginia Central between RF&P (Hanover) Junction (now Doswell) and Richmond, which would throw all our rolling stock and machinery into General McClellan's hands should he defeat Lee. Like all other fights nobody knew what the result would be. I know our railroad president, Colonel E. Fontaine, and Superintendent H.D. Whitcomb felt much anxiety as to how it would end. The government was equally as much concerned in this matter of transportation, as the railroad men had already laid a track in Eight Street, from the old RF&P depot, corner of Eighth and Broad Streets, to the Richmond and Petersburg Railroad (now Atlantic Coast Line) depot, corner Eighth & Canal. The track was just laid down right on top of the street ballast and set up high and dry. This was the first southern connection ever made through Richmond and it of course gave an outlet for all RF&P rolling stock, but it did not furnish any relief to us down in "Butcher Flat", that is, at 17th and Broad Streets. We were in a hold, for a fact. Fortunately for all concerned, Superintendent Whitcomb was an experienced engineer. He had taken an active part in building the temporary track over the Blue Ridge mountain while the Blue Ridge tunnel was under construction.

One Sunday afternoon while we boys were all gathered in the corner room of the large brick building, corner of Broad and 17th Streets, Superintendent Whitcomb came in looking serious. We knew something was the matter. Walking up to the front window, which looked out upon Broad Street and through which we had for an hour or more watched the pretty girls going to and from church, he said, "Boys, we must get our engines and cars up that hill or we will run the risk of going into the army, for if General McClellan gains the victory, he will clean us up of railroads." We soon found he was in dead earnest, and early next morning, having gotten permission from the authorities to lay a track from our 17th Street track to the RF&P depot, corner 8th and Broad, we soon had Broad Street full of cross-ties, rails, etc., and a very large force of laborers.

He had Mr. Stephen Hunter, general freight agent, and all the depot forces, the 17th Street shop carpenters and of course all the trackmen working on it. He was much laughed at—The idea of running an engine up that hill!—and was of course much abused for obstructing the street, Mr. Whitcomb, however, very soon had the track laid, connecting it with the 8th Street track, corner 8th and Broad. The grade will average 350 feet to the mile and in one place, at intersection of Jail Alley, it must be 375 feet or over to the mile. To make sure of this grade I have had the city engineer give me the figure from his office. At Broad Street and Eleventh the street level is 160.50 feet above the tide; the distance from 17th to 11th Streets is 1,950 feet; and engines had to raise 131.31 feet in this distance. At the intersection of 17th and Broad the street level is but 28.99 feet above the tide. The up-hill Broad Street track intersected our 17th Street track with a Y running out east on Broad Street so that the engines backing down from the roundhouse into the Y would switch front into the Broad Street track. The engines were brought down for trial. The excitement ran high. All of the city, government officers and all, came out to witness the experiment.

The old Millboro, built in 1857 by Norris and Sons, was the first engine to make the trial. Engineer Fendall Ragland was not then the nervous old man he is now. (That is, in 1892). He soon had the Millboro headed into Broad Street and an odd sight she looked to all. Mr. Whitcomb showed anxiety. He had Yard Master Dandridge Lowry and a force with "checks" to place behind the wheels to prevent the engines running back down the fill should they fail to go up. Mr.

Lowry told Ragland to go ahead. The old ten-wheeler took out up the hill at a pretty good rate until she struck the highest part of the hill at Jail Alley; then she commenced slipping her drivers. The fire flew. We placed the "checks" and held her fast, but never an inch would she budge further up. "Just as I said," could be heard all around. Ragland kept cool; he told Mr. Lowry to remove the "checks" back and let him try her a short distance lower down. Same result. By this time though, Ragland found he could let her back. He told them to take the "checks" up and let him go back, which he did, and backing as far back into the east end of the Y as he could, he sent for Mr. Whitcomb, who came to him at once looking mortified and disappointed. Ragland told Mr. Whitcomb that he must either run her up the 17th Street track to pump her up or run her up the hill. Mr. Whitcomb replied, "Why, Ragland, you have just tried and failed, so you had better let some of the other men try her or try their own engines, but if "Millboro" won't go up, none of them will".

This nettled Ragland, and he said firmly and determinedly, "Mr. Whitcomb, if you will throw them "checks" away and let me have my own way. Mr. Whitcomb granted him his request, cautioning him, "By all means don't burn her, but put out the fire just as soon as you get up the hill." The men heard what passed and stood aside to see her launch. Ragland gave her a good oiling; he crept down under her and examined her machinery quickly. Crawling out, and wiping his hands with the waste, he patted the Millboro and said, "Well, old girl, you and I will be in H— or at the Powhatan Hotel in ten minutes!" He slipped up and pulling her wide open, she bounced up and jumped on the unsurfaced track, and by the time she got to that tight place in the grade, she had gotten such a swing that the old clumsy thing shot up to the top of the sharp grade.

The track being laid on the top of the street ballast, as the engine rose, she looked to us, down in the bottom at the 17th Street depot, as if she had concluded to wing Ragland in a heavenly flight instead of that down grade he threatened her with before starting. The shouting crowd having followed up the hill, we soon saw the old Millboro standing in front of the Powhatan Hotel, with a crowd of curious spectators standing around her. The hotel proprietor, Seammell, told Ragland that as soon as he could leave his engine, to come down into the bar, as one of the servants had found a bottle of old rye in the lumber-room and he wanted Ragland to help him hide it.

At that time the government had a strict prohibition law in Richmond. It was the only time in my life of 55 years that I ever loved and drank whiskey, but to get it, and drink it on the sly was so funny and the whiskey was good. But to explain about "finding the bottle". The barkeeper had a dark room in the basement of the old Powhatan. He had a couple of bricks loose in the partition wall between his room and the old "lumber-room" through which opening he would pass the bottle to the middle man who would give out that he had found "a bottle of rye in the old lumber-room. The bottle was taken care of and the finder rewarded and the "dark horse" too.

The next engine which was up was the Whitcomb, which was built 1856 by Tredegar Works in Richmond. J.W. McClandish was engineer and soon all the engines were up. It only needed what our present energetic Master Mechanic, T.S. Lloyd, tells his engineers when they complain of their engines not pulling a certain number of cars on certain grades: "Give her the swing before you strike the tight place."

Soon all of our engines and cars that were on our Richmond end and were up on Broad Street or about on the RF&P or Petersburg side. Remember this was all prior to the battles, and now that the fortunes of war had left us in possession again of our road, we headed at once all of our rolling stock back down the hill. In getting the cars back, some cars got loose near the RF&P depot and took a half-mile flight down to 17th Street. They came like lightning, hitting broadside against a car which happened at this moment to be standing in the street, lifting it entirely off the wheels and throwing it around into the vacant lot south of Broad Street.

Yardmaster Lowry could say more funny things. Walking up to the box car as it lay on its side, end toward the track, and seeing it was not much broken, he remarked as he turned and looked at the mess of wheels, etc., in the middle of the street: "Old lady, it's well you did get out of the way."

Mr. Nathan Wildman soon had the 17th Street shop on double

duty day and night, getting ready the machinery and coaches to carry the army to Northern Virginia. The government was pressing our officers for unbroken transportation—Richmond to Gordonsville—which brings us back where we left Thomasson building the bridges.

The road was soon in status quo to Staunton, Va., and how we were able to see from the depot the Blues coming down those little mountains—and many silly and ridiculous occurrences such as only war can produce, I will have to tell you later.

# CHAPTER V

## On The Move Toward The Valley

Excuse my delay in fulfilling my promise to tell about how we managed so rapidly to move the armies of Northern Virginia with our very limited motive power and rolling stock during the campaign of 1862.

While General Lee was keeping one eye on General McClellan on the Bay, and the other on General Pope in Piedmont, we Virginia Central men were busy rigging our troop trains; bluff old Master Mechanic Wildman was all business—"No time now for foolishness," was his oft-repeated injunction.

Right in the midst of all this the shop struck, and nobody could blame them. Up to this time wages had run on pretty much as they had before the war, while notwithstanding our victories, every kind of living had gone up, so that our men could not support their families, so they determined to take chances of going into the army or getting more pay. They all came down to the general office, 17th and Broad Streets, two abreast. It was a sad sight, but very soon they broke rank and cheerily went back to the shops, their petition for more pay having been granted by Superintendent H.D. Whitcomb and President Edmund Fontaine.

As an illustration of how our wages compared with the cost of living—we had a jolly passenger conductor named Wm. D. Gilkeson, who one pay day, about that time, bet our ticket agent, Wm. F. Adcock, that he could go to a restaurant and eat up at one meal Adcock's month's salary. A big crowd gathered near the old market restaurant, and Gilkeson fairly won the bet, coolly requesting Adcock to send him fifty cents more for a common cigar. Granted. We soon had ready eighteen trains of about fifteen cars. There were freight cars of all descriptions, with one passenger car at the rear of each train for officers, the conductor riding there also, and acting as rear brakeman generally. Some of the army had already been hauled to Gordonsville and skirmishing had brought the line of battle, with General Pope, near Cedar Mountain. Then it was that General Lee's main army leaned forward in that direction.

It was generally very short notice we would get of army movements. Hearing the drums and seeing the mass of men and muskets moving to the depot was the first positive information we would generally get as to any military move. So it was in this case. Standing at 17th Street depot and looking toward the west, as far out in Broad Street as the eye could see, we watched the mass of confederate soldiers bearing down upon us, until, as they got near to the depot, the crowd grew so dense, and it was so hot, that it was almost impossible to keep them in order. However, when we would get the wrong soldiers off a train, and the brigadier-general would call for certain regiments to be loaded on certain trains, they would settle down on it as bees upon a hive and once down nobody was silly enough to give a soldier any advice as to finding better accommodations here or there. They were "There to stay." We gathered them in for ten miles along the road from Richmond, in the direction of Gordonsville. All trains loaded, we would pull with about ten minutes' space between trains.

Getting to Gordonsville, the first train would pull up and unload, and pull by until all the trains came in; then we would turn the engines around and start out to Richmond for another load. So we kept going for about ten days, during which time we never undressed, nor saw a bed. We slept some, while waiting for other trains to load or unload—engineers on their boxes, we on the cars. I wish now that I had counted how many soldiers would pile into one train. How tenaciously they would stick! On top of a slanting woodtop car or wherever they would find room enough just to hold on, they would stick. To illustrate: We loaded all the trains one evening and started from Richmond to Gordonsville, just about dark. Going out from Richmond we always had a tough tug to get over a summit about four miles from the City. That night was no exception to the rule. We all got in sight of each other, while going up this grade; but after turning the grade and getting on what our "Uncle" Jimmie McClandish called

"Our side of the hill" (down-grade), we endeavored to get our ten minutes' space as soon as it was practicable to do so. We had rolled along down toward the Chickahominy for about two miles, when entering the very heavy curve around Strawberry Hill our engineer called sharply for brakes three times, and reversed his engine. After running back to give the following trains the signal, I ran up to the engine to see what was the cause of his signal. I found our engine Albemarle, so near the rear of the preceding train that her headlight cast a ring of light about the size of a hogshead on the rear of the coach ahead.

I saw the men under a freight car. The drawhead had pulled out, dropping one end—the end that was fast prying up the floor of a luggage car that was literally packed with soldiers. The officers were all asleep, and those soldiers so worn out and so sound asleep, that we could do nothing with them. We tried to show them the danger they were in, and how narrowly they had escaped being crushed. We begged them to transfer to the other cars, so that we could throw out of the train this broken car and put it into the little side-track near Chickahominy, which the bridge carpenter built there to put the pile-driver on when at work on the trestling. It held about two cars. The few soldiers who did wake sufficiently to make any reply only ridiculed us. I never before heard such nonsense talked as I did that night. They heard us say something about the draw-head. "Draw-head," said one soldier, bawling out, "Draw your heads out o' here, or we will draw them for you."

The hole in the floor which had been caused by the draw-head bursting through, they called, "Ventilator," "Head-rest", "Elevator," "Jess let her set", "Jess let her go like she is." "Let her roll", etc. I asked them to move so that I could get room to stand in order to nail down the floor which was torn up. Looking at my brogan shoe, one of them remarked to me, "Stranger, ain't you mighty unhealthy?"

It was very trying to me just at that time, bothered as we were with a dozen trains waiting, but being in his power, I answered politely, "Not particularly so, sir; why do you ask me that?"

"Nothing, Captain, more than I see that most of your body lies on the ground and I always heard 'twas so unhealthy to lie on the ground. Well, boys, let's move and let the Captain have enough room for one foot."

John Davidson, the engineer of the damaged train, proposed that we quietly put the broken car, soldiers and all, into the little pile-driver track, and leave them there—a very wise solution of the difficult question. We very soon carefully placed them in, cut loose and coupled up to the rear cars and pulled out for Gordonsville. What became of those soldiers, whether or not they got back to Richmond or got on some other soldier train the next day or deserted, this deponent knoweth not. We were never questioned about it, either by our railroad officials or by army officers. The crowd of soldiers at Gordonsville the next morning was so large and mixed that the car we cut out did not check short. It was "railroad bliss", as the soldiers called it, and they passed by as unnoticed some little irregularities in our management.

On my next trip out from Richmond the regular engineer of the engine, Albemarle, which had been pulling my train, was unable to run her out, and in his place was detailed from the shops a machinist named "Dock" Galloway. I am not afraid to say that a machinist is not necessarily an engine-runner. During that night, with "Dock" Galloway as engineer, we became surrounded by circumstances peculiar and thrilling, and it was by mere chance or good fortune, if you choose to call it, that we escaped a fearful accident, before relating the detail of which, it is necessary to show the relationship existing at that time between our military and our railroads, and how it came to do so.

While the Confederate government itself was always very respectful to our railroad officers, and very seldom interfered with their managements, our Southern Officers would sometimes, especially during the first year or so of the war, attempt to assume command of our trains. To illustrate: It was in 1861 a train load of Southern soldiers came to Charlottesville, from Lynchburg over the Orange and Alexandria Railroad (now Southern). It was noticed that two soldiers rode in the cab of the O&A engine, and it seemed had the engineer under arrest, or rather under their charge. Our Virginia Central Railroad, of course, took charge of the train at Charlottesville. Our engineer, Ragland, running Monticello, asked the engineer on the

O&A what those two soldiers were doing on his engine. He replied that the Colonel put them on at Lynchburg. "And," said he, to Ragland, "They will take charge of you before you leave."

Ragland replied that he might be arrested but he swore he would run no engine under arrest. Sure enough, when his engine hooked on to the soldier train and while Ragland was greasing her up, etc., the soldiers entered the cab and took their position as they had on the O&A engine. Ragland climbed up on his engine and said, "Gentlemen, it is contrary to rules for anyone to ride on the engine. You must go back into the train."

They answered him that their Colonel had commanded them to ride there and to take charge of the engineer until he landed them safe at their destination. Mr. Ragland went straight to the telegraph office and got the operator to telegraph Superintendent Whitcomb that he was under arrest and that he positively refused to run an engine under such circumstances. Very soon came orders to the Colonel not to interfere, but to leave the transportation to the railroad officials. The soldiers got off and Ragland got on and pulled out.

One more illustration: It was early in the spring of '62 just before or about the time of the battle of Seven Pines, that there suddenly arose urgent necessity in the Peninsula for some soldiers that were yet in some part of Virginia north of Gordonsville. At any rate, there pulled up at Gordonsville bound for Richmond at 8 p.m., a double-headed train full of soldiers, with some refugees among them—women and children. It had been arranged for this O&A train to go right through, with O&A engines and men. We had a train also to come in as a section, either in front or near of this train. A dispute arose between Fred A. Kuper, our conductor, and Mr. Johan Fisher, Assistant Superintendent, of the O&A road, as to which train should take precedence. It ended in a fight and everyone got into a bad humor; and, or course, while squabbling where there was plenty to drink they soon got to drinking but the O&A train took the lead, however, with the engines "Jeff Davis" run by Amos Woodward and the "Nelson" run by one of the O&A engineers.

The "Jeff Davis", was captured from the Loudoun and Hampshire in 1861, with two others similar to her in build—the "Beauregard" on our road, and the "Johnson" on the RF&P road. They were three as nice and as smart engines as I ever knew. The engines were returned to the Loudoun and Hampshire road after the war and may yet live. Surely it would be interesting to know what fate befell noble refugees.

To return to my narrative. The orders received by the conductor of the leading O&A train were: "Come to Richmond—moments are hours." A Louisiana colonel was on the engine. He was about half drunk, and told Amos not to stop anywhere but for wood and water, and to "let her roll." Amos wanted nothing more glorious than such orders from the railroad officials and the military men telling him to go ahead and stop for nothing.

After sending these orders to this train at Gordonsville, necessity arose to start a train out from Richmond to Gordonsville, which left Richmond about 11 p.m. with orders to go to Hanover Junction and report. The train dispatcher considered this perfectly safe, thinking that he, of course, could intersect the fast east-coming train certainly at Beaver Dam, and knowing that all trains were ordered to stop at Hanover Junction—that was a standing order and very strict rule for both roads.

The fast-flying east-bound train came on by the Beaver Dam signal without even slackening up. The operator immediately informed the Richmond officer, whereupon the operator at the Junction was urged to stop the train at all hazards. Anxiously did our faithful train-dispatcher pace the floor waiting to hear the Junction operator call and tell him he had stopped the train. He did soon call, but alas! to tell the sad news that the fast Richmond-bound train had passed and not even slackened, but had crossed the old RF&P RR as fast as the engineer could run. The dispatcher's heart sank within him and he calculated where the trains would meet. He predicted that it would be in the curve at Little River. So it happened. Five minutes after passing Hanover Junction, the "Jeff Davis", with her ten passenger coaches literally crammed with soldiers with some refugees, amongst whom were some ladies and children, locked horns with old Millboro engine, a 10-wheel heavy freight engine run by the oldest engine-runner now living in the United States, Seth Mack, John H. Richardson

*A Typical Scene At A Railroad Station In The South*

was the conductor.

Seth was at a great disadvantage, being in a cut, and with a heavy left-hand curve. But he caught a glimpse of the Jeff Davis headlight in time to shut her off and to roll off into the sand. He knew better than to be found about that time, and he and conductor Richardson ran off quietly into the pines, made their way to Hanover Junction and reported the accident to Richmond.

This was the worst collision that ever happened on our road. How any mortal being could come out alive from some of these coaches was the wonder of all who saw the splintered wreck. Coaches were telescoped in every conceivable way, part of them hanging over the Little River bridge. There were many killed, among them a little child in its mother's arms, while the mother was not hurt at all. The "Jeff Davis" rebounded when she struck the "Millboro" and stood with her front truck off in the ditch and her boiler front all smashed. She looked like some wild beast which had been demolished by old "Millboro", and then dashed aside. The old "Millboro" was standing on the track but stripped back to her cab. It was soon after this that the circulars were issued by the Government forbidding any military officer to interfere with the railroad management unless he had positive instructions from the General commanding the armies. These circulars were posted in every station, engine cabs and cabooses, and prevented what, as I will try to show you soon, would have been serious accidents.

# CHAPTER VI

## From Richmond on a Soldier Train

Resuming my narrative of our hurrying the remainder of General Lee's army from Richmond to reinforce Jackson, who had gone to Gordonsville to meet General Pope, I will tell you one of my trips out from Richmond with a soldier train.

Mr. John M. Kroft, the regular engineer of the "Albemarle", was called to his family, and the master mechanic detailed a machinist named "Dock" Galloway to run the engine.

As I have said before, a machinist is not necessarily an engineer. However, expert and competent he may be as a machinist, it requires experience for him to learn to handle successfully engines and trains in emergencies and under difficulties. Put a healthy 22-year-old boy on an engine and let him there learn the thousand and one difficulties that necessarily come in the path of a train runner, as, for instance, those that befell Galloway that night of which I tell. It is not down in the books, this knowledge, but it has to be driven in my hard knocks, and once in, cannot be lost. It seems to me that some of our old runners have such a mastery of the machine that they appear only to watch the track ahead. A first-class locomotive is to machinery what the lion is to beasts—the kind. Nobody can blame ambitious young men for falling in love with an engine, for it is the picture of life itself. But to my story.

Dock Galloway was a small, nervous gentleman, very polite and quiet, as good and harmless as he could be. I was right glad to see him on the Albemarle when it backed down and coupled on to my train successfully with Galloway as with some others. We took some officers aboard in Richmond, and got orders to load soldiers between Chickahominy and Hanover—the soldiers who had come to the railroad via the Cold Harbor Road. The cars were soon crammed full of soldiers, of course, inside and out, and we got along very well during the day, keeping pretty well up with our preceding train, which, fortunately, as it turned out, was in charge of Conductor

Joshua Finks and Engineer John Davidson.

About 8 p.m. we got safely in Melton's Station, about four miles east of Gordonsville, and having turned over the Summit there, rolled along down a 65-foot grade which runs nearly all the way from there to Gordonsville. Feeling that we only had to let her roll on into Gordonsville and being anxious to reach there and rest, we forgot to tell our new engineer of the wayside woodpile where we usually had to stop and get wood.

Oftentimes during the war we had to stop at out of the way places to get wood from the ricks along the road. It was very dangerous and was the cause of right many accidents. Running into the cut of Cain's Old Field, Engineer Galloway gave one sharp whistle for down brakes. I listened anxiously for the second blast, which would have meant, "Stop!", as one blast was often only intended to slacken speed. I was, of course, on the lookout, and saw our rear dash past a red lantern and I also got a glimpse of a mess of folks in the ditch. I did not care to run over the tops of all these freight cars loaded with soldiers but decided to see why it was that Mr. Galloway did not call for brakes again, reverse his engine and stop the train. I signaled my brakeman and called to them to put on brakes on every car ahead of me the rear of Fink's train, which was just moving off from the woodpile where they had stopped to get wood and had sent the red light back to stop us. I can never forget the scene, made forceful by the powerful light which the "Albemarle" headlight threw on the train.

The soldiers who were on top of the rear officers' car scampered ahead for the front cars, thinking that we had run into them. Captain Finks in rear of his train waving his lantern with all his might, the door of the coach open and the headlight of our engine revealing all excitement therein, and all on the rear platform.

But John Davidson made the Westward Ho spit fire as she coughed and snatched from the jaws of death two trains full of soldiers. It was certainly a happy disappointment to us all that John kept ahead and prevented the Albemarle from smashing into the rear coach. What on earth was the reason that my engineer, Galloway, did not do anything to stop his engine, under such circumstances, I could not imagine unless possibly he had fallen asleep, not being used to running and being out at night.

I tugged on over the soldiers until I got to the front of the front car and looking down into the cab saw, alas, that it was empty!

The soldiers sat in front of the cars with their feet hanging down like boys on a goods box.

"Where are the engineer and fireman?" I quickly asked one of these, who replied, "Pshaw, they both jumped off when they saw that light yonder, Cap", continued they, as I was getting down into the tender to get over into the cab, "You'd better mind; we heard those officers on the train in front halloo back that they will shoot every road man on this train when they reach Gordonsville."

My first impulse was to give the engine steam in her reversed condition and come to a full stop, to see what had become of Galloway. But the thought then flashed into my mind that the train following us had by this time gained on us, as we were running very slowly. I leaned out of the cab and heard it coming, evidently having turned the summit, I at once threw her in front gear, whistled "Off brakes" and pulled out for Gordonsville, choosing death to myself in front rather than death to my train of soldiers and myself too in the rear.

I fully believed that I would be shot at Gordonsville by the soldiers before I could explain the situation, and show them I was innocent.

Pulling into Gordonsville, going west, there is, after passing the last county road crossing, a straight line almost a half mile along, which runs up nearly to the east switch at Gordonsville. We were just coming around the curve into this straight line when I saw a red and white lantern coming rapidly toward me and waving us to stop. I, of course, called for brakes reversed and stopped. Good Captain Finks, pale and trembling as he came up out of breath, seeing me as I leaned out of the cab to learn of him the trouble, "Carter, you will all be shot! for God's sake run to the woods!" he cried. "Where are Galloway and the fireman?" I quickly told him what had happened. While in this state of excitement we heard the following train coming along around the curve back of us. Instinctively, I must say, for I hardly knew what

I was doing, I whistled "off brakes" and pulled the engine open, intending, certainly, to get far enough into the straight line for the following train to see me in time to stop and let me pull out of their way.

Conductor Finks pulled himself up on the engine and we got almost in sight of the station yard at Gordonsville, when I concluded to stop and take care of Number One. The soldiers in the front car, seeing and hearing it all, had become very much interested and said to me: "Captain, stand your guard; you saved our lives and we will try to save yours," and they began to load their muskets.

"Let's run up to the station and tell the officers all about how it happened."

Captain Finks said, "That's it, boys, come on". And they ran up the yard to the depot, while I with peace commissioners in front and bayonets and balls in the rear for my defense, sat serenely on the "Albemarle" and was soon assured by Captain Finks and his confederate officers that it was all right with the soldiers. I pulled up to the reception room as meekly and mannerly as I possibly could.

What on earth had caused Galloway and the firemen to jump off where they did was the next question. It was a mystery to all of us. Captain Finks and Engineer Davidson agreed to take care of our train and a great crowd of us got lanterns and went back up the track to see what had become of Galloway and the fireman. Curiosity and anxiety were at their height. The old mountain country road and the railroad run alongside from Louisa Courthouse to Gordonsville, a distance of 14 miles, and never lose sight of each other. It is a curious fact that Contractor Elisha Melton located the railroad, running the levels with three sticks, and built the road, a slab track, the western extension of the Louisa Railroad, about 1840. Notwithstanding the fact that it was built without the use of an engineer's instrument, the grades and curves remain just as "Lisha Melton" located them fifty years ago, and it now forms a part of the great C&O system. But to my story.

I only intended to say that in order for us to go down the railroad we had also to see at the same time all that passes on the county road and some of our party soon met Galloway and the fireman both nearly dead, laid out in a two horse wagon, with "rack body" and poles put in to make a bed for the wounded men. The brakeman who had signaled Galloway to stop, and whose nonsense had caused the accident, stuck to them after finding them injured and secured the wagon which he happened to catch on its way home from the woods.

"Why did you jump?" was, of course, the first question. Galloway, it seems, not being an experienced engineer, and having heard so many exaggerated reports of soldiers bayonetting railroad men who caused collisions, thought that the red light was hung on the rear of Fink's train and that he was actually into the preceding train filled with soldiers, and so he jumped off after doing all he could to stop. The fireman jumped, he said, because Mr. Galloway jumped.

We used then a square tin lamp, the back tin, the sides white lights, and a red glass in front, but the red glass had a tin door over it to open and shut on a wire hinge. The brakeman said that the tin door would not stay open, so he put it up against his breast and kept it open with one hand perfectly still. That was what fooled Galloway.

Dock never pulled another throttle open but being too disabled for war or railroad life, he assumed the more peaceful occupation of gunsmith, which he successfully carried on.

# CHAPTER VII

## Railroading at Waynesboro and Staunton

I am compelled to tell of the difficulties under which we railroaded in 1861-1865.

Well, boys, here is one of my trips in the early fall of '61. Being promoted from baggage-car to conductor of troop trains, I got orders to take a load of provisions from Richmond to Jackson River (near Clifton Forge), the then terminus of the Virginia Central, for the Western Army, which was as well as I remember under the command of General H.A. Wise. The train consisted of about twenty freight cars of provisions— no caboose. I rode sometimes on the engine and sometimes on the rear freight car loaded with hogsheads of sugar, bacon, etc. We had the engine Staunton, and John Harton, engineer. The Staunton was built about 1858 or '60 by the New Jersey Locomotive works. She was bought for a fast passenger engine. Her drivers were five feet six inches high. She set up high on her bearings. On account of our Blue Ridge and North Mountain grades, the Staunton did not prove satisfactory. She had a most powerful whistle, and that is the most you would say of her. She would slip her wheels like "Old Spinner". But on moderate grades she could fly. The Staunton, was, therefore, put into extra freight use. In other words she had to step down and give place to those of better build.

About that time that we left Richmond at this period of which I tell, two double-headed trains left Jackson River for Richmond heavily loaded with sick and wounded soldiers from West Virginia going to the hospitals. We got orders at Richmond to go to Gordonsville and report for orders. Gordonsville was at that time the most important military point in Virginia or the South. About noon each day there stood at Gordonsville long and crowded trains from four different and very important military points. It was a busy scene, and about the depots, for an hour or so, there was a dense crowd of officers, couriers, soldiers and sutlers going and coming from the battle fields.

Being an extra we had to remain there that day four hours

before we could get orders to go West. The old Staunton had become so hot that she was blowing off loudly, and John Harton, himself, had on more steam than his boiler plates justified. We got orders, though, about four or five p.m. to go to Greenwood and "meet two troop trains and then to go to Staunton and report for orders." When John Harton pulled up on old engine Staunton, I was closely following, and—well, I was seeing how he rolled those twenty cars along the light grades and very rough track to Charlottesville. But when the Staunton struck the 75-foot to the mile grade, she soon told Mr. Harton that she had on too many cars. So he left enough at Mechums River to enable her to pull the train, and we soon reached Greenwood, and too, the siding to await the arrival and passing of the two troop trains mentioned in the order. The first train soon came through Greenwood Tunnel and stopped for water. "When's the other train due to arrive?" I asked the man. "Left it at Staunton; it is closely following and will be here soon," they answered. Sure enough, not long after the first train had left I heard number two, as I thought it was, coming. It soon pulled down out of Greenwood Tunnel and stopped also for water. "Hello, George, where's your train?" I asked of George Pelter, the engineer who was greasing his engine, John Timberlake, while his fireman took water.

"I could not pull my train and left my cars at Waynesboro. I am on my way to Richmond to get another engine," was his reply.

I, of course, considered then that the road was clear, and that my orders justified me in going ahead, having met one train, and the engineer of the second engine telling me that he had left his cars, which of course I concluded were those of the second troop train, at Waynesboro. Thinking there was nothing else to come, I ordered my brakeman to change switch and told Mr. Harton to go ahead. "Why Carter," he said, "that was only an empty engine that passed. How is that?" I explained to him that George Pelter had to leave his cars at Waynesboro on account of his engine giving out "Ah! All right then," said John, and so we pulled out. As I had to see the switch locked, I pulled up on the last freight car and wave him, Mr. Harton, to go ahead.

Now, before I relate the accident—awful as it was, which soon followed—I will show how we misapprehended the orders. The engine, which we met at Greenwood and whose cars had been left at Waynesboro, was not the train number two in our orders. There was a train at Waynesboro which had no orders from the dispatcher to move but as the engine was out of order, the engineer concluded himself to run under flag behind the first section of troop train and ahead of second section, thus making three trains, or at least three engines, which we would have had to meet at Greenwood had the dispatcher known that Pelter was coming in with his engine.

So tugged away the old Staunton, and on came from the city of Staunton, facing us, the double-headed troop train full of wounded and sick soldiers. Seth Mack, the oldest engineer in America, now hostler in the Richmond Yard, ran the front engine, Albemarle, a fine Rogers engine. Coupled behind him was the Norris engine, Monticello, run by John M. Kraft. When the Staunton turned the summit at Afton, and pitched into the dip and very severe curve, just before entering the eastern portal of Blue Ridge tunnel, the fated troop train was cautiously—thank God! rolling down through Blue Ridge tunnel. The tunnel is straight, but curves so suddenly at eastern portal that it is impossible to see scarcely any track ahead until you are out of the tunnel. So when Seth Mack popped out of the tunnel, Staunton's great headlight met him full face to face, and not a hundred yards away. "Uncle Seth" says he whistled for brakes and drew her back. Mr. Kraft also reversed his engine, thus somewhat checking the very heavy train, so that when the Staunton dashed her brains out against the Albemarle it very slightly disabled the latter; but the old Monticello caught the blow as the train in her rear bursted into her tender and otherwise damaged her. What saved us from a more fearful accident was the caution which the eastbound double-headed train was taking before entering the very heavy curve on the hill overlooking the lovely Rock Fish Valley.

The curve there is so heavy that the guard rail is used as a safety. Although badly bruised, I was able to go to the front and found Mr. Harton not only not killed, as I had feared, but at work on his engine getting her in a condition to handle. The smoke from all three locomotives rolled into the tunnel as it would have been drawn up a chimney, and soon there arose howls and curses from the poor suffering soldiers who were stifling from the smoke, which had now gotten so thick that it was impossible to breathe. Fortunately, no one was hurt by the collision. Only the smoke was killing them.

"Get down out of the cars, boys, and put your noses near the ground," cried out the voice of Conductor Joshua Finks, as he came along the side of his train to see what had happened to the front. The sick and suffering soldiers actually got down into the water which continually runs through this tunnel, and thus managed to get breath and get out alive. The smoke was stopped just as soon as we could put out the fires.

The crowd soon gathered. Some officers, the attendants on the sick, and some furloughed soldiers came to where we were working on the wrecked engines. "Whose fault is this?" loudly called out an officer in a commanding voice. "Major, here are my orders," answered Conductor Finks, "Go to Greenwood and meet one troop train; go to Charlottesville and report for orders." This is the train I should have met at Greenwood," concluded he.

John Harton had in one hand an old-fashioned torch—black smoke and big blaze—and in the other his monkey-wrench. He realized the situation, and turning around said, with a firm and manly voice, "Major, I pulled out of Greenwood side track, where my conductor had the switch changed, and gave me orders to do so. But though I am innocent, I am as well prepared to die now as I ever will be, and if you will only allow me time to get my engine back to Afton side track, so that these poor suffering soldiers can get to the hospital, you can dispose of my old body as you please, for I am nearly dead, anyway", and turning away his smutty face we went to hammering again.

"Where's the conductor of this train?" boldly asked the major.

I was about to put my nervous fingers into my vest pocket for my orders and explain when good and witty old Conductor Finks answered: "dead, sir! mashed to death in the rear car among a lot of government supplies!"

"Yes," said John Harton, "And in hell, I hope." But John knew I was within ten feet of him as he spoke. Then, Captain Finks, turning quickly to me, said, "Henry, by the way, you must take a telegram at once to the Greenwood offices. We must have two engines here at once, and the wrecking forces to clear the track. These poor soldiers must be carried to the hospital, if we have to roll Old Spinner down the mountain to do it." At the same time walking me off and giving me his lantern, while he pretended to be writing a telegram. As soon as he got me far enough off he gave me a sure enough message, and told me to go to Greenwood, report the accident, and then keep out of sight until the soldier's train had passed. For once in my life, I can truthfully say, I took advice.

I joined my crippled train next day in Afton, but had to go to bed on account of injuries received from being caught between a hogshead and side of the car when the accident occurred. In about a week I reported to Superintendent Whitcomb at Richmond, who said to me, "Carter, had I seen you immediately after the accident occurred I would have discharged you at once, but your absence, on account of your being hurt, had given me time for reflection and I confess that my system of giving train orders was imperfect. I have now adopted a rule of giving in every train order the names of conductor, engineer and engine of both trains"—a rule which worked well and continued in use for twenty years. Continued my honest Superintendent, "You can go back on your baggage car with Conductor Jones. I would say traveling in trains crowded with soldiers is rather serious."

What happened to the troop train in the tunnel that night may seem impossible, but I can prove it if necessary, just by way of argument. From some cause there was in the troop train a flat. The flat was lower in body than the freight box car in rear of it and when the collision occurred the box car jumped entirely off truck on to the flat, and was carried, with soldiers in it, to Richmond, so nicely did it fit itself into the flat. Of course, it happened so.

# CHAPTER VIII

# The Blues Close In

It was March, 1865, General Sheridan had beat General Early back up the Shenandoah Valley, near Waynesboro. It was evident—and a very serious consideration it was—that if General Sheridan was allowed to pass Rock Fish Gap and cross over the Blue Ridge into the eastern portion of Virginia, that it would certainly affect General Lee's rear and his main source of supplies for his army at Richmond, where he was still waiting and watching the crouching lion, General Grant. Lee had no soldiers to spare to send to meet Sheridan, as all he could do now was to hold his own in front of Richmond, General Early, therefore, prepared to give battle at Waynesboro, and thus attempt to prevent the passage of Rock Fish Gap, one of the very few passages through the Blue Ridge. General Early very prudently held his supplies at Greenwood Depot, a station on the eastern slope of the Blue Ridge and just east of the last of four tunnels which lie between that point and Waynesboro. (This was written in 1894. Since then, C&O has relocated Blue Ridge tunnel and converted Greenwood tunnel into an open cut, as of 1944).

Waynesboro, is at the western base and Greenwood at the eastern. Two of our trains were held at Greenwood partly loaded, while a good many supplies were in the depot ready to be moved to General Early if he so ordered, or to be sent flying down the grade to Mechum's River if the god of battle so decided. One day, while there shifting, unloading and reloading commissaries, Captain A.D. Wren (1894: the father of our present C&O passenger conductor W.D. Wren) who was in charge of the commissaries at Greenwood, acting under Major H.M. Dill who wanted to move the supplies in great haste. The depot stands on a spur track about a hundred yards across from the main track. "Finks" said Captain Wren to Conductor J.B. Finks, who had charge of one of the trains, "I want you to take your engine and run over to Waynesboro to carry whiskey to General Early's men. I have just received an order to hurry it on, as a fight is expected soon. Just roll a barrel on the tender, back over to Waynesboro, put it out on the platform, and come right back. Don't get cut off there on the other side of these mountains and bridges."

"Good, sir," said Finks, whose family lived in Waynesboro, "I want to get a clean shirt anyway and tell the old lady good-bye."

Mr. R.W. Goodwin, his engineer, was informed, and soon got ready to load on a barrel of liquid fire. It was corded up with the wood in the tender of the Albemarle. It was a very fine engine, if it got good foothold, but would slip unless you gave her plenty of sand. The boys used to say that if you were to spit on the track old Albemarle would never go over it. As the engineer, Mr. R.W. Goodwin, will be the most prominent character in my narrative, allow me to say that this Christian gentleman still lives and earns his daily bread by pulling the throttle. He now runs the C&O No. 123, ten wheels connected. (This was written in 1894.) As an almost daily witness of this man's conduct for thirty years, I can truthfully say that his life disproves the oft-repeated assertion that a railroad man cannot be a Christian. His religion is recognized by us all, and no one would dare ask him to deny his Master.

Backward sneaked the old Roger engine through four tunnels and over Smith River bridge. When it came up to the platform at Waynesboro, Mr. James Wallace, the agent, took charge of the barrel. "Bob!" then said Conductor Finks, "I'll run home and tell the old lady good-bye and be back in ten minutes."

"All right," answered Mr. Goodwin, "But I am afraid Mrs. Finks will not let you return, as times are so squally around here. If you are not back in twelve minutes I shall leave you." "Just look here", suddenly exclaimed Agent Wallace, who was standing close to the Albemarle. "Finks, our men are defeated. Look up the road! Look how they fly!" No one can give a description of the sight of cavalry scout fighting that will do it justice. To see a road full of fleeing cavalrymen, then their enemies hotly pursuing, is something one cannot forget, but which cannot be described. It must be seen to be appreciated, and you had better be in the bushes, as I was, when you do see it. The best time made on this turf is not on record; it lies buried in the grave of the "Great Unknown."

But the fleeing cavalry made it. Conductor Finks saw aplenty, and hesitating a moment over the ponderous question which presented itself to his anxious mind, "Shall I desert my train and share the fate of my family, or leaving them to the tender mercies of the enemy, shall I save my train and commissaries?" Finally, with one foot on the platform steps of the Albemarle, he said to Mr. Wallace, "James, tell my folks I feel it my duty to go and save my train, but after I do that I will try to get back to them as soon as possible."

He now pulled up on the Albemarle and Mr. Goodwin needed no further signal to roll over the bridge, which, having passed, he took it slowly up the grades and around the heavy curve, where he had full view of the flying cavalry and pursuing enemy. When the Albemarle passed Afton, a station four miles east of Waynesboro, some of General Lee's cavalry had already passed, so rapidly did they ride. It was only a few minutes to Greenwood, where everything was on the move. One long full train of commissaries was standing down our main track ready to go. Conductor Finks and Mr. Goodwin were ordered to run in on the spur track to get the three cars, which had been loaded with supplies, out of the depot.

While shifting about there, news came that the Yankees were very near, and the firing could be heard. The long train on main track pulled out. The switchman, in the confusion, threw the switch wrong and derailed one car, but Engineer Goodwin, realizing the necessity of prompt action in order to escape, reversed his engine and gave her all the steam he had. Fortunately the car got back on the track at the switch. In double quick time the train, consisting of three cars in front of the Albemarle and four behind, was on the main track and headed east towards Richmond. Conductor Finks, who had changed the switch, pulled up on the engine saying, as he did so, "Bob, I am afraid they have got us." Mr. Goodwin pulled cautiously out of the eastern portal and out approach of Greenwood tunnel, and entering the open yard around the passenger office, exclaimed, "Great Heavens! Josh, we are gone", as he saw the Federal cavalry all about and around the depot and crossing. Conductor Finks, thinking, of course, that they were captured, jumped off from the opposite side of the engine from where the enemy could see him. The fireman, George Whiting, was colored, and the brakeman, Jim Cowling, also colored, all jumped off. Mr. Goodwin followed Captain Finks to the steps of the engine with the intention also of jumping off, but suddenly changed his mind, he concluded to remain and run the gauntlet. In the meantime the engine was rolling slowly toward and getting close to the enemy. Springing to the throttle, Mr. Goodwin attempted to open it wide and thus increase his speed and prevent the enemy from boarding the train. The throttle being hard to open, his effort failed, and so he ran by the cavalry at a rate not exceeding fifteen miles per hour. After his efforts to increase his speed failed, he fell to the footboard and stretched himself out like a lizard on a log in order to avoid being shot by a cavalryman, who, by this time, was riding by the side of the engine and trying his best to shoot Mr. Goodwin. But the engine and tender received the seven carbine bullets which were intended for Bob. One bullet severed the cushion seat, which was at this time unoccupied, and then punched a hole in the tank but too high to waste much water.

By the time the cavalryman had wasted his seven bullets the engine had arrived at a point where he could not ride further, on account of the termination of the high earth and stone platform leading from the passenger depot to the Dinwiddie Hotel, and upon which the cavalryman had ridden. Bob realized his advantage and did not fail to make good use of it. He again jumped to the throttle, and having made a strong pull, had the joyful satisfaction of feeling the machine respond to his touch, and under a shower of curses from the cavalryman the Albemarle darted on.

All old Virginia Central men remember the Albemarle's whistle and when Bob got clear off he gave his would-be captors a loud and long farewell. Mr. Goodwin will always attribute his escape to a kind providence, in whom he trusted, when he prayed as he did while the cavalryman's bullets fell harmless around him.

Any railroad man knows that an engine and seven cars, no brakeman, rolling down a 75-ft grade, will very soon attain a speed which is dangerous. Mr. Goodwin began to look around, realizing his still critical situation, and looking about for some of his crew, he saw a colored brakeman a green hand along the train from where the firing had come, clinging on the side of the boiler and holding to the handrail. He was frightened nearly to death. Then looking back in the wood on the tender he discovered Davy Spradling, the assistant depot agent at Waynesboro, who had secreted himself there to avoid capture. Mr. Goodwin soon had them both in the train and not a minute too soon, for it took a reversed lever, a full head of steam and all that the brakes could do to prevent a rear collision with the front train which had stopped in the mountain slope for wood. After leaving Pierre, the train reached Mechum's River, a station fourteen miles from the eastern portal of Blue Ridge tunnel, and the foot of the grade being 1,000 feet lower than Afton, which is near the said tunnel. Leaving Mechum's River still going east, Mr. Goodwin encountered a pretty stiff grade rising Ivy Hill.

He feared trouble, for he was out of sand. He soon became convinced that he would either have to cut loose and leave some of the cars there or he would be captured by Sheridan's cavalry, who were coming right along that way, the road which they took being in full view of where he stood spinning his drivers. He ran back, intending to cut off two cars of the rear of the train, but Captain Wren, who had charge of the commissaries, begged so hard that he should not do it, that Mr. Goodwin concluded to try her once more, and see if he could, by using dirt on the track, by this means get her to pull the seven loaded cars up the grade. If he could have had sand, it would have been no load for the Albemarle. With plenty of sand it could have pulled 18 cars up the grade. Mr. Goodwin became convinced that it was useless and dangerous to lose any more time and so he was obliged to cut loose the two rear cars loaded with commissaries and leave them standing on the main line.

When the Federal cavalry came by next morning they took off the brakes and let them roll on to Mechum's River bridge, a structure 75-feet high and 300 ft. long, and annointing bridge and cars with oil, burnt all to ashes. Mr. Goodwin rested awhile at Charlottesville, and then resumed his trip to Richmond, which he reached the third day from the time he left Greenwood, acting as conductor, engineer and fireman the whole way, 118 miles. Two young men who were assisting Captain Wren were killed at Greenwood as this train pulled away. Mr. Randolph J. Albemarle and a Mr. McCreary. Captain Wren and Mr. McCreary were crouched behind an iron safe in one of the cars; but Captain Wren said that McCreary lost his life by looking around from behind the safe to see what was going on against Captain Wren's caution.

Captain Finks was captured, but released by General Sheridan, after strenuous and persistent intercession of the citizens of Waynesboro. According to the custom on both sides in those days, however, he had to forfeit his watch and boots.

# CHAPTER IX

# Railroading Through the Raids

...The years 1863 and 1864 were years of raids. The Northerners—found out they could never whip us rebels so long as we could get bread; so they concluded to starve us out. Here in Eastern Virginia we had, in '63 and '64, the Stoneman, Kilpatrick, Dahlgren, Sheridan and other raids. By looking on any railroad map one can see that a raid into East Virginia from the north must very soon strike the Virginia Central Railroad. It lay broadside to Washington. The reader must remember that what during the war constituted the Virginia Central Railroad, running from Richmond, via Gordonsville and Staunton to Clifton Forge, and whose locomotive equipment consisted of 26 little woodburning engines of from ten to eighteen car capacity, now forms a part of the great Chesapeake and Ohio system, with the name being changed to Chesapeake and Ohio Railroad Company as of August 31, 1868. It took fifty millions of New York money to adopt the little old Virginia Central and rechristian her. As to whether Mr. Huntington and his New York conferees, who furnished these millions, ever got their money back, or ever wanted to, it is not my province to know or discuss. I can only say for their comfort, that the strongest tie that now unites the west and east is the C&O cross-tie and heavy steel rails.

It will also be seen by reference to the map, that the Gordonsville end of the road made this portion the most exposed during the war, from Hanover Courthouse to Gordonsville; and this happened to be the very portion which was General Lee's main dependence for transportation of his army and supplies. This important fact, of course, attracted still further the attention of the Federal military, and they continuously sought, and repeatedly accomplished, the destruction of the bridge, track and depots, which were all more or less filled with General Lee's army supplies. The Virginia Central Railroad, connecting with Orange and Alexandria via railroad at Charlottesville, was the main feeder for General Lee's army. So highly did he appreciate the importance of this road, and its necessity for his army, that once when our superintendent H.D. Whitcomb, resigned on account of some interference on the part of the military, General Lee made the position of our superintendent Whitcomb a military necessity and commissioned him with the title of Major. He also issued an order which we boys gladly posted in our caboose cars, tenders and telegraph offices, that no officer or soldier under his command should in any manner interfere with the management of the railroad, or dictate as to the modus operandi. All during the war our general yardmaster was Cornelius Tyler. He was nearly as well known as any man in Lee's army. 'Neal Tyler, as he was familiarly called, was fond of the "Pomp of Office." The officers gladly allowed him the honor even of being general manager so long as he was willing to assume, also, the responsibility, worry and trouble incidental to the honor. Neal liked it all, except sometimes it got too hot for him. He kept one of General Lee's orders pasted on his hat.

Just here I cannot withhold a little incident which illustrates "Neal's love of official position and sense of humor, as well as the great demand upon our 26 little locomotives and meagre equipment during the war. That these little old woodburners played a most important part in crowning the Confederacy with victory time and again cannot be questioned. That no historian has ever given to the railroads their just measure of honor, is but an additional proof that from the public they zealously serve, they must always thus expect large blame and no praises.

It was in '62 just after the Seven Days' fight around Richmond when we were busy transferring General Lee's army from the vicinity of Richmond to Gordonsville to Meet Pope's army. Trainmaster Tyler had just loaded out every available engine and car, and feeling greatly relieved of this burden, he had taken a sociable drink at the Antilotta barroom in the passenger room at the depot. He stepped out upon the pavement to view the cleared-up yard and saw, coming down Broad Street, a cavalry officer, who rode almost up on Tyler and demanded to know where he could find the superintendent.

"I am he, sir," said Tyler.

"Well," said the officer, authoritatively, "I want ready here in 20 minutes three trains of 20 cars, to load up with those soldiers now coming down the street!"

Tyler coolly and in a dignified tone, replied, "Well, General, I have already sent out every single engine and car that can turn a wheel. But alight and be seated. I'll go up at once and order Master Mechanic Freeman to build three engines and have Master Car Builder Childs put up sixty cars and have 'em here in twenty minutes."

The officer dismounted and after most civil inquiries learned that his men must go foot-cavalry in the direction of Gordonsville until they would meet the empty trains returning and be taken up by them.

These cavalry raids were always greatly exaggerated. The terror and consternation that preceded them in many cases did more harm than the actual presence of the soldiers. The points oftenest raided were Atlee, Hanover Courthouse and South Anna Bridge, the latter five times burnt, and five times rebuilt, and standing when Richmond fell, Beaver Dam depot was raided once in '62, once in '63, and twice in '64; Frederick's Hall and Louisa Courthouse each twice. It is a remarkable fact that Gordonsville was never captured from us during the war. In '62 General Pope got in sight of it, but we ran Jackson's division into the town just in time to see the Blue uniforms coming down the little mountain, and they soon disappeared, making a stand and giving old Stonewall a desperate fight at Cedar Mountain.

I will tell you about the Kilpatrick-Dahlgren raid, which came in from Frederick's Hall and crossed near Beaver Dam; as I know it from personal experience, and from the experience of eye-witnesses and participants personally known to me.

The raid upon and the burning of Hanover Courthouse depot by about 100 men from Stoneman's command was May 4, 1863—about the time of the fight at Chancellorsville. The raiders came from the direction of Fredericksburg, bearing down on the King William side of the Pamunky until opposite Hanover Courthouse, then crossing over and heading directly to Hanover depot. They reached there about night and completely destroyed the depot and several cars, all full of army supplies.

Mr. James D. Christian was the railroad agent there then, and lived in a company building about 50 yards from the depot. Mr.

Christian had a happy family consisting of a wife and five beautiful curly-headed daughters and one little son. They were all seated at supper in the basement of their dwelling, in sight of the depot. Mr. Christian had two servants, Aunt Maria and her daughter. These were the house servants and what our colored people call "White folks' niggers." Presently and suddenly the door opened and Aunt Maria came in. She stepped out into the middle of the floor and assumed that absent-minded, stiff, staring appearance—the indescribable and inimitable condition into which the genuine African gets when converted and relating his experience.

All eyes turned toward Aunt Maria and the girls began to laugh, "Hep you'sef, Mars Jim. Hep you'sef, Miss Ellen. Hep you'sef, young missies. De Lord done come and I am free."

"Oh, do pray, Maria, go along and let us finish supper," said Mr. Christian. Just then Aunt Maria, who was waiting on table, happened to look out of the window toward the depot, cried, "Law, Mars Jim, what white folks is dese?"

Mr. Christian jumped up, and seeing the whole depot yard full of cavalry—Federal—took the situation in at once. Turning to Aunt Maria, he spoke, "The Lord is come you say? The devil is come, more like!" He then turned to his wife and told her that the yard was full of Yankees, and they were setting fire to the depot. "This house will certainly be burnt, as it is so near, and all the railroad property, too." said Mr. Christian. "Take the children and servants, and carry everything out of the house that you can and pile it up in the garden yonder. I will go out and beg the commander to spare the house."

In less than twenty minutes the old frame depot and several cars full of stores were ablaze. Mr. Christian humbly approached the officer in charge and begged him not to destroy the building.

"I was sent here, sir," he said firmly, "to destroy this property as a military necessity. My orders are, to burn all railroad buildings." The officer, in turning from the burning depot to speak to Mr. Christian, caught sight of Mr. Christian's garden. The furniture had all been dumped in the back part of the garden in a pile. Mrs. Christian and a half-dozen girls—her daughters and cousins—all the servants and all the dogs, were grouped together. The dogs all thought it was a frolic and so did the girls, who had gotten into a perfect glee. There the girls stood with their hair blowing to the breeze, and all curly-headed; there by them the nappy-headed negroes and the curly-haired dogs. The great blaze brought out this scene in bold display to the commander, and turning to Mr. Christian, he said, "Is this all your family?" "Yes," said Mr. Christian, "And I am their sole support. If you take away our house, we are out of doors."

"Well," said the officer, "The house shall not burn. I will order my men to protect it." He then took a good look at the scene and said, "If I could truthfully reproduce this picture and carry it north, there would be no more war." The officer then ordered his men to spare the house, and gave Mr. Christian some substantial proof of his humanity.

Little Willie Christian had followed at his father's heels, and hearing the good news rushed home to tell his mother that the house was spared. This produced a happy change of scene. Each person began to recover for herself her dear possessions and in the general chaos to find her special treasure. "Whar's my child at?" said Aunt Maria, suddenly remembering that she hadn't seen him since the excitement began. "Where's my new hat-box?" cried Mrs. Smith, Mr. Christian's married daughter. She had just gotten this new bonnet in Richmond and it stood first in her affections. "Here's yo' band-box, Sue," cried one of the girls. "And horrors! Aunt Maria, here's yo' baby in the box on top of Sue's new bonnet!" Nothing could have been more ridiculous and the fun of the girls waxed fast and furious, until Mr. Christian, not knowing the cause of the fun, came up and said, "Come, come children, how can you do so, under such distressing circumstances?" But one glance and he too joined in the fun. In half an hour, every soldier had gone and nothing but the huge pile of smoking embers, casting their weird light against the sky, was left to speak of their visit. Such is one experience from a cavalry raid.

# CHAPTER X

# Raids Around Richmond

The Kilpatrick-Dahlgren raid, February 29, 1864, in sight of the Confederate capitol, and between it and the main army of defense, being entirely unexpected and announced by even the firing of a gun, was, to the military and citizens of this part of Virginia, the greatest surprise of the war. On March 1, when General Kilpatrick crossed the South Anna River at Blunt's Bridge, 23 miles from Richmond—and about which I will write later—had he gone directly toward Richmond, instead of going around to the east of Richmond, he could very probably have taken the city easily. For, by doing this, he could have reached there and made the attack on the Brook Road, at the same time that Colonel Dahlgren did on the Westham Road, and before General Hampton, who was in his pursuit, could have overtaken him. But anyone can see it all after it is over.

This raid awoke from Winter's lethargy not only the peaceful citizens, but also aroused the dogs of war and put in action both armies, which, up to this time, had been wintering on their respective sides of the Rappahannock River. General Grant assumed command a fortnight after the time of which I write and soon after fought with Lee the historic battles of the Wilderness, Spotsylvania, North Anna River, Hanoverton and last, but by no means least, the bloody battle of Cold Harbor, which, in my humble opinion, was the most severe repulse General Grant ever had.

I was a prisoner at General Grant's headquarters, a short distance from the battlefield, on the evening of the last great battle of Cold Harbor, and I formed this opinion from what I saw and heard from the soldiers around "Bull Ring" as they called it. We were under guard. Such significant orders as these were given, "No lights! No Fires! No loud talking! If there is any demonstration among the prisoners, the camp will be shelled! Place the cannon to bear on the camp, etc." No so-called coffee was made that night in our tin cans, but in silence we nibbled our hard tack. One of my fellow-prisoners, having in his possession a small piece of meat, and overcome by the desire for the flesh-pots of Egypt, had raked a few coals of fire together, and was essaying to make unto himself a little savory stew, in which his soul delighted. He was complacently stirring the concoction and humming to himself in sweet anticipation, when a guard came quietly by. With a gentle movement of his foot the guard kicked over the stew and firmly crushed out the coals. Not a word was said on either side. It was the "Sublime eloquence of an act." Words would have been idle!

Very early the next morning, General Grant moved rapidly, his army under cover of his gunboats at West Point, on the York River. History, however, tells this.

General Kilpatrick as he, with 5,000 troopers, approached Anderson's Ford, on the North Anna River, about two miles from Beaver Dam depot, on the Virginia Central Railroad, while Colonel Dahlgren, with less than 500 men, crossed the North Anna ten miles higher up the river, opposite Frederick's Hall depot, on the Virginia Central Railroad. General Kilpatrick struck the Virginia Central at Terrell's Crossing, about one and a half miles east of Beaver Dam depot, where he came very near capturing the train of which I was conductor, and of which I will presently tell. He did not harm the railroad track. I will here remark that these raiders did no harm to property; they took, as they went, the sleds and horses; but they did not tear up and destroy track, as General Sheridan invariably did.

From Terrell's Crossing General Kilpatrick went across the country to Little River, encamping for the night on Colonel Fontaine's farm, called "Colley Swamp". Then, crossing Little River at Honeyman's Bridge, and the South Anna at Blunt's Ridge, he went in the direction of Atlee, on the Virginia Central, northeast of Richmond. He encamped near Atlee on the night of March 1, 1864, and was attacked during the night by General Hampton, routed, and made his way back to the Federal lines the next day. Colonel Dahlgren crossed the Virginia Central tracks about two and half miles east of Frederick's Hall, at Gunnel's and Coat's crossing. His men were in two squads. They captured a court-martial which was in session in an old house on Addison Coat's farm, mounted them on Mrs. Holladay's horses and struck out for Dover Mills (now Sabot) on the James River, crossing the South Anna at Car's Mill. Finding that he could not ford James River at Dover Mills, as it seems he had been informed by his guide, Colonel Dahlgren took the mountain road north of James River and pushed toward Richmond, approaching the capitol on the evening of March 1st via the Westham Road. When a few miles from the city he met the Local Defense Troops and fought the sharp battle of Glenburnie. In passing, I will say that the Local Defense Troops were composed of employees of Tredegar Iron Works, the armories, the railroad men, department clerks, etc. Before this battle our Local Defense Brigade, under the command of General Custis Lee, was the laughing stock of the army. Many funny predictions were made by both military and citizens as to what would happen were these defenders forced into a fight. But this battle placed our Local Defense Corps alongside the gallant boys who wore the gray. One drawback to our Local Defense Brigade was their proximity to Richmond and the accessibility which the boys had to a city's many temptations, attractions, and snares. To resume, after this battle of Glenburnie, Colonel Dahlgren evidently decided to get back into the Union lines, as General Kilpatrick had failed to signal him. Colonel Dahlgren came out on the Brook Road and crossed the Virginia Central at Peake station and crossed the Pamunky River at Hanoverton.

Having given in dry facts an outline of the raid as a military movement, I return to my narrative. On the day that General Kilpatrick was approaching the North Anna River at Anderson's Ford, opposite Beaver Dam, on the Virginia Central Railroad, Dr. Charles J. Terrell, a Confederate surgeon, and G.N. Thompson, a Confederate cavalryman, both of whom lived near Beaver Dam, and who were then at home on furlough, had agreed to go across the river into Caroline County to take a hunt, intending to cross at Anderson's ford. At 2:30 pm on the same day, February 29, 1864, I left Richmond for Gordonsville with the afternoon passenger train, consisting of one baggage car, one express car and three passenger coaches. The engine was E. Fontaine, built by Norris and Son, 1854. It had four drivers, 60-inch diameter and was run by Engineer James Ramsey. (This engine exploded at Wickham's station November 14, 1864, instantly killing

James Ramsey and an unknown soldier who had just flagged the train to get on, and was struck when just opposite the exploding engine.) The train was crowded as was every train during the war, with citizens, soldiers, sutlers, etc. The E. Fontaine was a fairly good passenger engine for those days and James Ramsey not a timid driver. As we dashed along through Hanover County that afternoon we had as little idea of what a dangerous trap was then set for us to fall into as did Dr. Charles Terrell and "Galley" Thompson, familiarly known as "Galley." They were riding toward Anderson's ford and "Galley" had just been talking over his shoulder to Dr. Terrell, telling him what a narrow escape he had once made from being captured. As they approached the river he threw the reins on the horse's neck to let him drink. At that instant Kilpatrick's men, who happened to ride up on the opposite side of the river, covered him with their guns and called, "Surrender!" "Galley" was so surprised and startled that he dashed his loaded gun over his head into the river and cried: "The damn Yankees have got me at last." The men then took him in charge and carried him along near his own home. Seeing a neighbor, "Galley" called out regardless of the personality of his remarks, "Tate, tell Lucy Ann—his wife—the damn Yankees have got me, but I'll be home to dinner tomorrow." Sure enough, that night he dug himself out of a tobacco house where he had been imprisoned and got home the next day to dinner!

Dr. Terrell was far enough behind Mr. Thompson to take in the situation at the river and to save himself. He retreated in good order, going back to Beaver Dam, notifying them and hurrying home near Terrell's Crossing, he put one of his servant boys on his finest horse to reconnoitre and report to him the situation of the enemy. He never again saw horse nor rider. Meanwhile, he had another boy "hook up" the oxen and haul the meat into the woods. "Save your bacon" was, literally, "first in the hearts of our countrymen"—and women too—whenever we heard of a raid. Dr. Terrell was hurrying the boy and oxen along, so as to get the bacon safe and in a hiding place before he left the house, when he heard my train coming at Hewlett's station three miles off. He realized that we would be captured or killed if we went on, so he determined to try to notify us of the danger. Accordingly, he left everything to the care of his wife, and started out for the track. He ran down it some distance hat in hand, and waved us down. Ramsey seeing him, called sharply three times for brakes, which meant trouble, so out of the window popped every head, to learn the cause of the signal. We then saw Dr. Terrell running up and waving. We wondered what the trouble could be. "What's the matter, Doctor?" we called out, as he, exhausted, came up to us. He answered at once, "The Yankees. They are between here and Beaver Dam. I saw them not a half an hour ago myself. They are certainly trying to capture your train, for I heard the cavalry riding rapidly down the county road. They are riding toward Hewlett's in your rear, to cut you off." He begged us to run back as quickly as possible, warning us that we would otherwise certainly be captured very soon. Turning quickly to Ramsey, I said, "Jim, what's best?" "Cap'n," said Ramsey, coolly, "I'll do anything you say; but dam if I believe there's a Yankee this side of the Rappahannock River." The doctor again assured us that he had seen them himself but he added, "You'll soon see!" Hotly discussing the matter, we walked a little way up the track toward where the enemy was supposed to be, turned the curve in the track and emerging from the curve and the woods, we got a view of about half a mile across the fields. The discussion ended there. We saw the dismounted cavalry coming in line out of the woods on the opposite side of the field. They caught sight of us and as their bullets began to sing that short-metre tune, Dr. Terrell said, "Ramsey, are there any Yankees this side of the Rappahannock?" "Yes," answered he, "and if we don't get away from here, we will be on the other side of Rappahannock!" We thanked Dr. Terrell for saving us, and telling our invitation to join us.

  Never was "Get aboard" said more hurriedly nor obeyed more promptly than then. More quickly than I can write it, we were under full swing, running backward, regardless of all rules to the contrary, almost as fast as the engine could turn her wheels. I ran back through the train with my negro brakeman, Daniel, and in this reversed condition of our train, he and I took the respective positions of fireman and engineer. Watching out ahead, we ran out into a field where the country road runs parallel to the railroad a distance of about half a mile from the track. We saw this road full of cavalry officers who were riding at full sweep. We naturally took them for the enemy and as they were ahead of us, we feared they would make the Hewlett's crossing first. The passengers took in the situation and got down between the seats, giving the inside of the train the appearance of the Methodist churches during prayers fifty years ago. (They don't get down that way nowadays—too upright!) Brakeman Daniel hung down from the bottom step of the car, on the opposite side from the cavalry. He kept looking back under the coach, apparently at the truck. I feared rapid running had broken something, so I called out, "What's the matter, Daniel?" I soon understood, however, it was a case of not loving the truck less but Daniel more, for he was bringing the coach timber to bear between his body and the enemy's bullets. We had to stop at Noel for water and as we were then four miles from the enemy, as last seen, we ran curves a little less recklessly. Soon, reaching RF&P junction, we wired report to Richmond. We got orders to "Shift train and come to Richmond. Road is clear. Dead-head all passengers with tickets west of Hewlett's." We afterwards learned that the cavalry whom we nad raced were the Maryland Cavalry, like ourselves, on a stampede.

Referring once more to our friend, the kind Doctor. After seeing us safely on our way to our train he started on his way home through the woods. Just as he was about to jump the fence which let him into the main road a soldier rose up and met him. Dr. Terrell had the advantage, having his pistol well in hand. He raised it, aimed and was about to fire when the soldier threw up his hands. "Friend!" said he. "Open that Yankee overcoat, then!" said the doctor. "Ah!" he continued, "the Maryland line?" "Yes," replied the soldier, and the "glad hand" was given by the Doctor, who took his captured friend home with him.

The fastest time ever made is undoubtedly not on record. It was when a cavalry man on a Government horse heard the word, "Go", and knew the price to be his life. Watching him at a distance and his pursuers in sight made the horse appear like the little tin horses the boys have, with their legs stretched straight out before them and behind. One peculiar thing a retreating cavalryman would do was to stop and shut a gate and put a peg or gravel in the latch. If he could do that and get his distance before his pursuers got to the gate he was all right. If the curses of Federal cavalry on those gate-latches that "push-down" instead of "lift up" had "come home to roost" the gates all through the North would never move. Naturally, every Federal soldier thought the latch must be lifted, and when after tugging and cursing he discovered that the latch needed only a light touch downward to open the gate, his game had flown.

On the evening of the raid we lost no time in obeying orders to come on to Richmond, stopping only at Hanover Courthouse to notify the people there. My young wife was then boarding near there, and I sent word I would be home some way just as soon as I got rid of my report which the War Department received of the raid, I am not prepared to say, but it probably was from the fact that General Hampton, who was then encamped at Bowling Green, Caroline County, started in pursuit of General Kilpatrick about Midnight of February 29.

Fulfilling my promise to my wife, I was at Hanover Courthouse the next morning by nine o'clock, having gone up on an extra passenger train which left Richmond on the time of the regular train to accommodate some Hanover people and some military who wanted to get information in regard to the raid. The train remained only long enough to catch up some cars that were at Hanover and load on what provisions could be gotten and returned to Richmond. Just as soon as the train left for Richmond there came over old Hanover Courthouse that awful stillness, indescribable, which prevailed wherever a raid was anticipated. Every sound heard and every horseman seen approaching, in our imagination, was the forerunner of Kilpatrick. There was nothing to prevent his coming to Hanover and we all expected him.

But this letter is already too long. In my next I will attempt to tell whether or not and how our expectations at Hanover Courthouse were realized; of Hampton's attack upon Kilpatrick at Atlee late at night; of the meeting of Colonel Dahlgren with Dr. Thomas E. Williams, a Confederate surgeon, who had the Federal wounded in charge, etc., etc.

*NOTE:*

*Three great grandchildren of Dr. Charles Terrell reside in Louisa County Virginia. His great grandson, Edmund A. Terrell III, of Frederick's Hall, is in possession of Dr. Terrell's medical case which contains medicines and surgical instruments he used during the war. His great granddaughters are Elizabeth Terrell Marshall of Louisa and Dorothy Terrell Dunkum of Green Springs.*

Dr. Charles Terrell, M. D., Colonel, CSA. Confederate Surgeon.

# CHAPTER XI

## Hanover Courthouse is Raided

In regard to the Kilpatrick-Dahlgren raid, in Virginia, February 29, 1864. This raid opened the military movements of that most eventful year in which our soldiers met and settled forever, we hope, upon the field of battlement, what statemen, trammelled by the technicalities of legislative enactments, had failed to adjust satisfactorily. We realized by practical experience, what we had hitherto regarded as sentiment, that "United we stand, divided we fall."

In my last letter, we had reached Hanover Courthouse. It was the morning of March 1, 1864. The momentous question was, "Where is General Kilpatrick?" He had crossed the Virginia Central Railroad at Beaver Dam and the evening before, headed for Richmond. Consequently, he was expected everywhere and by everybody in Goochland, Hanover and Henrico Counties. How to entertain the unexpected guest, was a question which gave his anxiously awaiting hostesses great concern. The farms, full of life at other times, would appear deserted when a raid was anticipated. Cattle were hid in the bushes, and bacon and other valuables were stuck away in every conceivable place. My young wife, during a certain raid, put $40 in gold under a setting hen. Men would be either bushwacking or hid in the houses, and sometimes the oldest woman in the family would answer the call at door or window. It was a saying down here that "a dog never barks at a Yankee cavalryman." Whether the rattling sabre makes the ravenous cur slink away or whether it was a Yankee trick, we never knew; but the fact remained. Such a state of things existed at Hanover Courthouse the morning of which I write.

The old Hanover Courthouse tavern was kept by Mr. and Mrs. Clivis Chisholm. Two more original, odd and funny pair rarely marry. Mr. Chisholm was a very small and nervous man, while Mrs. Chisholm was a large, good-natured lady, and had a plenty of good common sense besides. This old tavern was, during the latter part of the war, filled with refugees from those parts of the Eastern Shore which were then held by the Union armies. Mrs. Chisholm really ran the hotel, "Clive", as she called her husband, being willing to leave it all to the "Old Woman". In politics, Mr. Chisholm, like his distinguished neighbor, Mr. Wickham, and many other of our best citizens, was a Union man opposed to secession. In fact, Virginia herself was opposed to it, and it is, of course, recognized as a historical fact, that, could Virginia have remained neutral, she would never have seceded. Earnest, thoughtful and long were the sessions of our Virginia Convention during the winter of 1860–61. Virginia does nothing rashly. Every important step she has ever taken has been the result of careful deliberation. Thus was she considering the very important matter of secession when there came Mr. Lincoln's call for 300,000 troops. Then the die was cast and our many men of many minds joined heart and hand to do battle a la mort.

But to return to the old Hanover Courthouse tavern. Mrs. Chisholm, not knowing which army might come first and realizing that Mr. Chisholm, in his excitement, might make some impolitic and harmful statement, decided to put him away in some safe place. Nobody quite knows even now where that place was; but some assert positively that he was hidden between two feather beds. Then assuring him that she would meet and answer the officers, she marched bravely to the front. It was about ten o'clock in the morning. As she looked down the Hanover County road lane, as far as eye could reach, the road was full of cavalry. She did not know whether they were Northern or Southern troops; but recognizing the safety of neutrality she snatched up the first white thing she saw. It proved to be her grandson's nightshirt. This she fastened to a stick, and placed it conspicuously in front of the bar-room. "If they be Union, we are Union; if they be Southern, so are we," said the diplomat to herself while her flag of truce waved—its arms—proudly in the breeze. Beneath this she proudly took her stand, and bravely awaited the cavalry troops, who approached nearer and nearer—a General and his staff in front. The lady boarders were all assembled behind Mrs. Chisholm. They were not so exposed as she, but womanlike must see and hear.

"Good morning, Madam," said the Commander, as he lifted

his hat. "I am General Hampton. I am looking for the Yankees. Where are all of your menfolk?" "All that are any account are in the army, sir," promptly replied Mrs. Chisholm. "The others are all at the depot. There are none here." Being so much relieved at this turn of affairs the hostess offered to prepare the General some refreshment. But he courteously declined. The ladies all surrounded Mrs. Chisholm now and looked with delighted eyes upon the noble General and his gallant troops. "I must go to the depot and find out about the road, and then to Richmond," said the General. He then took a good look at the old Courthouse, which was built in 1735, and which is still standing intact. He moved on. Huddled together around a stove in Barney Briell's little store at the depot were about a dozen of us.

Hanover Courthouse has been Andrew J. Wingfield, from some unknown cause called "Colonel". This title was not from any military service. If he was ever brevetted on the field, it was for shooting birds. He was, and still is, a great hunter, and his prowess in that respect is undisputed. He suffered recently a loss in the death of his dog, Blackey. Shortly after the last election, some friend was regretting his defeat in the close run which he gave Dr. B.L. Winston, for the legislature, and the Colonel replied "Pshaw, I don't give a d--- for the legislature, if I only had Blackey back!" Well, the Colonel was one of us in the store that morning and Mr. Robert Doswell, county clerk, and others. We were discussing matters military and were every minute expecting to hear some war news.

"Hallo!" called a commanding voice in front of the store. Every eye was turned to the glass in the upper part of the store, through which we could clearly see that the front yard was full of cavalry troops.

"Kilpatrick's men!" said somebody. Barney Briell, who had been sitting on the counter, with one motion fell quietly backwards and rolled out of sight under the counter. All the rest of the crowd, except myself, ran out through the back door and down into the culverts under the Virginia Central Railroad, and some hid in the ditches in the meadow near the store. I got into such a fit of ridiculous laughter at Mr. Briell and at the foolish way we all did, that I gave up all hope of escape and sat down under the end of the counter, with my eye on the door, awaiting my fate. The door opened gently, and a soldier put his head in, saying again, "Hallo!" I then got up. "We are citizens," said I, "and in our own house." The soldier opened the door and came in. "General Hampton is out here", said he, "and he wants to know about the road from here to Richmond."

Before I could speak, Mr. Briell jumped up, and over the counter he went, running out to where the General sat on his horse. He soon, however, got so confused in trying to explain the roads to General Hampton that he stopped his explanations, and calling a youth who stood by, he said, "Willie, run down the hill yonder and call Andrew Wingfield. He can tell all about the roads better than I can. Willie, tell him it is General Hampton and his men."

Willie went running down the hill, calling at the top of his voice, "Oh, Colonel Wingfield, Colonel Wingfield!"

The Colonel, who was in the railroad culvert, here put his head partly out and said, "Hush, hush, you little redheaded devil! Don't call me "Colonel" now. Call me anything—call me, grandpa."

"Well, grandpa," said Willie, "General Hampton wants you to tell him about the roads."

In five minutes fully twenty men and boys rolled out of the culvert and ditches and were soon surrounding General Hampton, telling him all about the roads and the spokesman was our Colonel—not Grandpa—Andrew Wingfield.

From Hanover Courthouse, General Hampton went onward toward Richmond, via the roads which would have taken him over the Brook Pike; but when he reached Booker Hazelgroves' store, about ten miles from Richmond, where the road from Atlee comes into the Richmond road, he learned that Kilpatrick had gone on toward Atlee. Consequently Hampton turned in pursuit, going toward Atlee, and arriving there about midnight of March 1st, he and his staff stopped at Atlee station. It was a cold, snowy, sleety night. General Hampton, hearing that reflected light had been seen in the woods below Atlee, sent Colonel W.H. Cheek. Second North Carolina Regiment Cavalry, to see if it was the enemy and if he found that it was, to make the attack. The North Carolina Cavalry soon came upon the pickets and exchanged shots. The Federal pickets retired, but must have failed to report, as Colonel Cheek's men went within fifty yards of the fires. One hundred and fifty sharp-shooters of First National Carolina Regiment were in front and were under command of Captain Blair. They were ordered to lie down, and McGregor's battery opened fire. As soon as the first gun was fired, the sharp-shooters, rose, yelled and charged the camp, surprising them and causing a stampede, and capturing 150 prisoners, many horses and equipment.

Dr. Thos. E. Williams, surgeon, Second North Carolina Regiment, was ordered by General Hampton to take charge of the Federal wounded. There were 150 prisoners, 200 horses, saddles, bridles, blankets, pocketbooks, etc. Among the wounded prisoners, all of whom were well equipped, was an officer from Michigan. He made so much ado over his suffering that General Hampton told Dr. Williams he must go at once and attend to the man. The doctor thought from his cries of misery he must be mortally wounded. He begged the doctor to try to save his life. Dr. Williams began at once to examine his wounds. In the course of his examination, he found buckled around the man's waist, a very fine money belt; telling the officer he might as well give him the belt, the doctor proceeded to find the extent of his wounds, which were not serious and so he told the man. This intelligence quieted the wounded soldier but tightened the grip he had on his rich belt. A few days afterward, Dr. Williams had occasion to call at the Richmond hospital to see his prisoner-patient, whom he had sent to this hospital. "Tom Williams," said he "I did not know you were such a fool!" "What do you mean?" asked Dr. Williams. "Why, whoever heard of any surgeon dressing the wounds of a prisoner who had on a belt with $2,000 in greenbacks and not first relieve him of his belt!" Only the fact that the genial doctor expected to be married in a month prevented him from committing suicide. The doctor, to this day, grieves over the wrong treatment of that serious case.

But I must go back to the night of the battle. Confederate States surgeon Thos. E. Williams, of the Second North Carolina Cavalry, to whom I am indebted for the details embraced in this part of my narrative, was ordered by General Hampton to take all the wounded prisoners back to Booker Hazelgroves' store, which was on the main Richmond road, so that they could be cared for there and be in a convenient place to be removed to Richmond hospital the next morning. Dr. Williams says he filled the ambulances with the worse wounded and rode ahead to Hazelgrove to have fires lighted in the rooms before the ambulances got there. He had that done, and was coming out into the road to meet and help the wounded prisoners out of the ambulances and into the house. Whilst listening down the Atlee road for the ambulances, he heard cavalry coming up the Richmond road, and they were very soon upon the ground.

"Who are you?" demanded a cavalryman in front of the squadron.

"I am Dr. Thos. Williams, Confederate States surgeon, in charge of the Federal wounded prisoners, captured by General Hampton's command near Atlee a few hours ago."

The cavalryman dismounted, and taking Dr. Williams by the arm, escorted him across the road, remarking to an officer on the opposite side of the road, and who was talking to the wounded prisoners in the ambulances, which had in the meantime come up, "Colonel Dahlgren, I have a prisoner here for you."

Colonel Dahlgren turned toward Dr. Williams, under guard and said, "Who have you there?" Dr. Williams answered, "I am Dr. Williams of the Second North Carolina Regiment, in charge of the Federal soldiers wounded in the battle near Atlee."

Colonel Dahlgren courteously conversed with Dr. Williams for several minutes, getting all the information he could about the battle and situation of things pertaining to the movements of General Kilpatrick and General Hampton. "Well," said Colonel Dahlgren to the guard, "We'd best leave Dr. Williams here to take care of those wounded men. What do you think of it, sir?" said he to Dr. Williams. Dr. Williams, in the happiest manner, answered, "That would surely be the very best thing you could possibly do, and I assure you," continued Dr. Williams, "that I shall do my best to take care of your people and have them very soon placed properly in Richmond Hospitals." Dr. Williams begged of Colonel Dahlgren the favor of retaining his horse, which request Colonel Dahlgren granted. "One more favor", said Dr. Williams, "will you please not allow this house (which was by this time surrounded by Colonel Dahlgren's men) to be pillaged as it will require all the stimulants here for your wounded men?"

Colonel Dahlgren not only granted this request but sat there on his horse until nearly everyone of his men moved ahead on the road leading to Peaks Station, on the Virginia Central Railroad.

Dr. Williams wishes it put on record that Colonel Dahlgren treated him most courteously.

Asking Dr. Williams, just before he bade him "Good morning" what he thought of his—Colonel Dahlgren's—prospects of making his way, Dr. Williams told him that "it seems to be very unfavorable", so far as he was able to judge and bade him goodbye.

Again referring to how richly furnished were the soldiers of General Kilpatrick's command, how completely they were surprised, and demoralized by the unannounced night attack of General Hampton whilst they, tired and worn out, lay around their campfires asleep, that cold, rainy, sleety night, in the woods near Atlee. The next morning after the battle, the whole neighborhood picked up such valuables as they could find which the fleeing cavalry had lost, and which our men had not time to find nor cared to lug. One poor but highly respected lady found a purse full of greenbacks. She was so delighted that she told everyone. One of her neighbors kindly—for he had no idea of defrauding her—told her that he would exchange Confederate money with her for the greenbacks. She, still more delighted, gladly accepted his offer, thanking him for his kindness. Another neighbor, better posted on the currencies of the two contending governments, told her that she had made a great mistake. "You go right over," said he to her, "and ask him to let you have the greenbacks, and you give him back the Confederate money and bring the greenbacks to me." She took his advice. She soon returned with the greenbacks. "And now," said she to her friend, "I want you to buy that piece of land," telling him about which land it was, to whom it belonged, and how badly she wanted to have it. So he took the money and went at once to see the owner of the piece of land and asked him what he would take in greenbacks for it.

"I Don't care to sell it," said the owner, "for greenbacks, but I'll take $1,000 in Confederate money, cash, for the place."

"All right," answered the lady's friend, "I'll take the place and will be here with the money day after tomorrow." He took the greenbacks to Richmond and got in exchange for the greenbacks $1,050 in Confederate money, which he paid to the owner of the land, got the deed for the property and gave it to the lady. When her husband, who was a Confederate soldier, returned from the war, she had a home for him, upon which they have lived ever since, and have raised a large family of worthy sons and daughters. "It's an ill wind that blows nobody good."

# INDEX

## A
Addison Coat's farm, 60
Afton, 45-47, 50, 52
Albemarle, 32-33, 38-39, 41, 45, 49-52
Anderson's ford, 60-62
Atlee, 56, 60, 65, 70, 72-73
Atlee's station, 24, 70

## B
Barney Briell's store, 69
Battle of Glenburnie, 61
Beaver Dam, 14-15, 24, 35, 56, 61-63, 67
Beaver Dam depot, L, 24, 56, 60-61
Beaver Dam station, 24
Blue Ridge, 3, 9, 25, 43, 48
Blue Ridge Tunnel, 3, 25, 45, 48, 52
Blunt's bridge, 59
Booker Hazelgrove's store, 70-71
Bowling Green, 65
Broad Street, 2, 25-26, 28, 30-31, 55
Brook Pike, 70
Brook Road, 59, 61
Bull Ring, 59

## C
Capitol Square, 21
Caroline County, 61, 65
Car's Mill, 61
Cedar Mountain, 31, 56
Chancellorsville, 56
Charlottesville, 2-4, 6-7, 15-16, 18-20, 33, 44, 46, 52, 54
Clifton Forge, 43, 54
Cold Harbor, 38, 59
Confederate Capitol, 59
Cowpasture River, 24

## D
Dinwiddie Hotel, 51
Doswell, 20, 25
Dover Mills, 61

## E
Eastern Virginia, 54
Exchange Hotel, 18

## F
Forest Hill Church, 16
Fredericksburg, 1, 20, 56
Frederick's Hall, 12-14, 56, 60, 66
Frederick's Hall depot, 60
Frederick's Hall station, 24
Frederick Harris, 12

## G
Greenwood, 44-48, 50, 52
Greenwood tunnel, 44, 48, 50
Goochland County, 67
Gordonsville, 4-5, 14, 16-18, 21, 23, 29-31, 33-35, 38-41, 43, 54-56, 61
Gunnel's & Coat's Crossing, 60

## H
Hanover County, 62
Hanover County Road, 68
Hanover Courthouse, 9, 22-24, 54, 56, 65, 67, 69-70
Hanover Courthouse depot, 56
Hanover Junction, 21, 35-36
Hanoverton, 59, 61
Henrico County, 67
Hewlett's station, 62-64
Honeyman's bridge, 60

## I
Ivy Hill, 52

## J
Jackson River, 43
James River, 19, 25, 61

## K
King William, 56

## L
Little River, 35-36, 60
Local Defense Corps, 61
Local Defense Troops, 61
Louisa, 5-6, 10, 13, 16, 66
Louisa Courthouse, 5-6, 8, 15, 41, 56
Louisa Railroad, 12, 41
Lynchburg, 2, 33

## M
Malvern Hill, 21, 25
Mechum's River, 3, 48, 52
Melton, 16-18, 39
Mineral City, 11

## N
North Anna River, 59-61

## O
Orange, 2, 54
Orange & Alexandria Railroad, 33
Orange Courthouse, 4, 17

## P
Pamunky River, 56, 61
Peaks station, 73
Pierre, 52
Powhatan Hotel, 27-28

## R
Rappahannock River, 59, 63
Richmond, 1-3, 6, 8, 12-15, 20-21, 23-25, 28-29, 31, 33-36, 38, 43-45, 47-48, 50, 52, 54-56, 58-61, 64-65, 67, 69-72, 74
Richmond, Fredericksburg & Potomac Railroad (RF&PRR), 1, 20
Richmond, Fredericksburg & Potomac depot, 25-26, 28
Richmond, Fredericksburg & Potomac junction, 20-21, 25
Richmond & Petersburg Railroad, 25
Rivanna River, 19-20
Rock Fish Valley, 45
Rock Fish Gap, 48

## S
Seven Days' Battle, 20, 22, 25, 55
Seven Pines, 34
Shadwell, 18
Shadwell Mills, 19-20
Shenandoah Valley, 48
Smith River bridge, 49
South Anna bridge, 1, 20, 22-24, 56
South Anna River, 1, 9, 24, 59-61
Spotsylvania, 59
Staunton, VA, 29, 43-45, 54
Strawberry Hill, 1, 32

## T
Terrell's Crossing, 60, 62
Tredegar Iron Works, 4, 28, 61
Trevillian, 16

## V
Valley of Virginia, 1, 8
Virginia Central Railroad, 1, 2, 8, 12-13, 25, 30, 33, 43, 51, 54, 60-61, 66, 69

## W
Waynesboro, 3, 43-45, 48-50, 52-53
Washington, 3-5, 8, 25, 54
Westham Road, 59, 61
West Point, 60
West Virginia, 21, 43
Wickham station, 61

## Y
York River, 60
Young's mill, 1